THE
HIGH LYSINE
AND FIBER
CANCER PREVENTION
COOKBOOK

THE HIGH LYSINE AND FIBER
CANCER PREVENTION
COOKBOOK

By Cory SerVaas, M.D. and Charlotte Turgeon

Fleming H. Revell Company
Old Tappan, New Jersey

Also by the authors:
The Fiber & Bran Better Health Cookbook
Benjamin Franklin 1977

Published by the Fleming H. Revell Company
Old Tappan, New Jersey 07675
by arrangment with
The Benjamin Franklin Literary & Medical Society, Inc.
ISBN 0-8007-1436-9

CONTENTS

INTRODUCTION

Why a High Lysine and Fiber
Cancer Prevention Cookbook?

The aim of this cookbook goes far beyond basic good nutrition. With it, we seek to reach toward an era of preventive medicine through diet, for "the wisdom of the prudent is to give thought to their ways . . . ." Proverbs 14:8 (*NIV*)

This cookbook offers dishes that match those of the greatest chefs for downright delectability. If we have sometimes compromised the strictest standards of a cancer prevention diet slightly, it is because we know that—no matter how healthful a dish is—if it doesn't taste good, you won't prepare it again. We have tried very hard to make these recipes tasty so you will use them often.

We want to help you prevent cancer, diverticulosis, hemorrhoids, gall-bladder disease, appendicitis and much more. It is now respectable to speak of preventing cancer with diet, thanks in part to the good work of the National Cancer Institute, which has given skeptics the hard evidence of a link between cancer and diet. One example of such hard evidence is the presence of *fecapentaene* in the stools of people who are on fiber-depleted diets and who have a high incidence of colon cancer. It is not present in the stools of fiber-eating populations, who are colon-cancer free.

At The Saturday Evening Post Society, we are glad that we did not wait for this hard evidence but began to alert our readers 15 years ago *that fiber could prevent colon cancer and many other afflictions*. Dr. Vincent DeVita, director of the National Cancer Institute, puts it this way: "Since we know that increased fiber intake seems to do good things for people, we can offer them information on fiber and then refine it as we go along, or we can wait until it is refined down to the 'nth' detail and then give it to people. I frankly don't see any reason to wait."

We at The Saturday Evening Post Society believe we are now at the stage in lysine research that we were with fiber 15 years ago. And so, as Dr. DeVita made the brave decision to urge increased consumption of fiber before all the figures were in, we urge you to increase your intake of lysine and to decrease arginine, even though the research is still under way and much is still not understood.

Lysine is one of the amino acids that make up protein needed for growth and for the repair of body tissues. Lysine is called an "essential" amino acid because it cannot be synthesized by the body but must be supplied by the diet.

When scientists speak of proteins, they often refer to the "biologic value" of a protein. By this term, they indicate how much of the protein is composed of the essential amino acids.

In famine-stricken nations, where the children develop *kwashiorkor*, the lysine and the other essential amino acids are pivotal. The shortage of essential amino acids is primarily responsible for the children's failure to grow. The low blood-serum protein of the protein-deprived children causes their protuberant water-filled bellies.

When given nine essential amino acids, the body can synthesize the other eleven amino acids necessary to make proteins. Lysine and tryptophan are the two essential amino acids most deficient in normal corn. In the more affluent societies, lysine and tryptophan are obtained from milk, meat and eggs. Food containing protein is fed to animals, and the animals (or their eggs and milk) are consumed. Meat, eggs and milk are, however, poor sources of fiber. Whole-cereal grains are a good source of fiber, but the protein they contain is often deficient in lysine. Rice, for example, has only a very small amount of protein, and that protein is relatively low in lysine. It has been reported that a child cannot eat enough rice to meet his protein needs—yet rice is the mainstay of the diet of much of the world's people.

Another large segment of the world's population lives on a primarily corn diet. Unfortunately, corn is very low in the essential amino acids lysine and tryptophan. When there isn't enough lysine and tryptophan, as in corn, the other amino acids can't be put to use as the building blocks for protein. Dedicated scientists and humanitarians, such as Dr. Edwin Mertz of Purdue University, have devoted their careers to improving the lysine content of corn so it can become a nearly perfect food. In the high-lysine corn they developed, tryptophan is much higher also.

Thus, for the poor in such countries as those in Latin America and South America where corn is the main (and often only) food, protein deficiency among both adults and children can be eliminated by substituting improved varieties for the corn seed they plant. Because young children require five times as much protein as adults per pound of body weight, diet improvement—especially important to future generations in Third World countries—has exciting implications for undernourished people throughout the world. For example, substituting high-lysine corn for rice in the diets of many Asian peoples would immeasurably improve their nutrition. Some countries now have programs encouraging their people to plant high-lysine corn rather than food plants yielding little protein or protein of low biologic value.

We believe high-lysine corn to be such a major nutritional advancement that it commands center stage in this cookbook. Not only is high-lysine corn a food with high biologic-value protein—it is an excellent source of food fiber. In this book, we have sought to provide many ways to use high-lysine corn in delectable dishes.

Other cereals can be good sources of lysine. In recent years, scientists have succeeded in crossbreeding wheat and rye. The resulting grain is called triticale. Several varieties of triticale provide protein of high biologic value, or higher than wheat, and this new grain can thrive where growing conditions will support neither corn nor wheat. Triticale, we are sure, will be important in coming years in the feeding of undernourished millions in the so-called Third World. Triticale has a delightful, nutty quality, and it tastes more like rye than like wheat. We have included in this book several recipes that call for triticale. If you want something new that is an adventure in good eating, try one of the triticale bread recipes.

Amaranth is another high-lysine grain for which we have provided recipes. Old rather than new, amaranth was called "the grain of the gods" by the Aztecs, who cultivated it along with the maize from which our corn is descended. Amaranth is a source of easily digestible, good-quality protein, and it is a good source of fiber. The tiny grains may be popped like popcorn, cooked to serve as a breakfast porridge or pulverized in the blender to make flour. See the amaranth recipes in "Test Kitchen Favorites."

Don't overlook barley. It is now available in a high-lysine variety. Because barley flour may not be on the shelves at your local market, you can make your own by putting a half cup of pearled barley in a blender for one to three minutes at high speed. See the new barley recipes in "Test Kitchen Favorites."

Over the past several years, scientists have learned a great deal about the herpes virus' behavior in the test tube. One of their discoveries is that lysine exerts a powerful restrictive action on the virus so its reproduction is blocked. They have also learned that just as lysine is essential for most animals, the amino acid arginine is essential for the herpes viruses to live and multiply. They found an antagonism between these two amino acids, chemically very similar, in the utilization of arginine by the virus. If lysine were present, the virus could not use the arginine. The virus apparently mistakes lysine for arginine, but when it incorporates lysine instead of arginine into its structure, it is incapable of reproduction.

A growing number of physicians are now using lysine in the treatment of mononucleosis, shingles and other herpes-related viral illnesses with good results. *The Saturday Evening Post* has received thousands of letters from people suffering from recurrent cold sores (herpes), who have noted repression of their infections while taking lysine supplements.

Many letters have come to us from people telling of cold sores breaking out after overindulging in nuts or chocolate. These are foods rich in arginine. Those who report the most success in keeping their cold sores from breaking out are those who take lysine supplements and avoid high-arginine foods. (Even gelatin in Jello® contains enough arginine to cause problems in some people.)

At the Post Society, we asked ourselves the question: If lysine is a safe, effective way to combat herpes viruses, might it not also be effective against other viruses? If it will fight a small "reptile" (herpes), we would like to try it on a "dragon" (cancer). Because some cancers have been associated with viruses, might a high-lysine/low-arginine diet be a possible way to prevent cancer? Our curiosity was aroused by the outcome of our cancer-prevention readers' survey. For the past four years, *The Saturday Evening Post* has published a health questionnaire to which nearly 20,000 people have responded. Among other questions the survey asked, "Did you develop cancer in the past year?" and, "Have you taken lysine supplements regularly?" As our computer tabulated the reports, one of the interesting findings to come out of these surveys was that those who took lysine supplements regularly had a lower incidence of newly discovered cancers than those not taking lysine. Of course we cannot ascribe cause-and-effect here, but we believe the finding deserves more inquiry.

To further test this theory, we secured 100 mice congenitally infected with mouse leukemia virus. The virus causes these mice to die of leukemia when they reach an average age of 267 days. These mice were divided into five groups and were given diets containing different amounts of lysine and arginine. At the end of a year, the mice on the highest lysine and the lowest arginine diet had a survival rate significantly higher than the mice on regular mouse food or of those on low levels of lysine and high levels of arginine.

The results of our first yearlong experiment were published in the November/December 1984 issue of Anti Cancer Research. The experiment is being repeated in our laboratories at the present time and, again, six months into the experiment, the mice on the high-lysine/low-arginine rations have more survivors than control groups.

But more exciting than the mice experiments is the mind-boggling potential of high-lysine corn for preventing *kwashiorkor* in children of all the Third World countries, where corn and other foods low in lysine content are the staple diets. The Nobel prizewinner Dr. Norman Borlaug, with the help of the Rockefeller Foundation, is evangelizing in South America to persuade farmers to grow high-lysine corn. A poor farmer in South America was heard to say, "A bushel of high-lysine corn may weigh a little less, but our children weigh more."

We want to teach our own population about the virtues of eating lysine (high biologic-value protein) in the form of grains and greens as the farm animals do so that we can avoid much of the high-animal-fat foods. You will create a cash market for it so that our farmers will be able to grow high-lysine corn for export to Third World countries, not to prevent cancer but to prevent death from *kwashiorkor*.

The word *kwashiorkor* literally means "the disease the baby gets when the next baby is born." The protein in the mother's milk is not replaced in his grain diet. Adults can survive with a lysine-poor corn diet, but the children can't. If they must eat a corn diet, they need our high-lysine corn to survive. This is the very reason that as many as 80 percent of the deaths in some Ethiopian camps are children.

In the meantime, we are hoping many of you will begin eating high-lysine grains because when you choose these, you get a meat substitute as far as high-quality, biologically good protein is concerned.

The high-lysine and high-fiber dishes in this cookbook are also intended to help you prevent high blood pressure and its consequences—heart attacks, strokes and kidney failure—by reducing the amount of salt you eat. And we hope to win you away from white bread that contains little fiber and lots of calories. Researchers have linked the use of refined white flour and refined sugar to a host of problems, including diabetes. When our "civilized" diet of white flour and sugar is substituted for the natural high-fiber diet common in more primitive societies, a whole catalog of ailments appears. On one small Pacific island, where sudden wealth led the natives to switch from a diet of yams and coconuts to one featuring white flour and sugar, 35 percent of the population developed diabetes.

Another aim in encouraging people to change to the high-lysine and high-fiber diet is to wean them from the high-fat foods shown to contribute to hardening of the arteries and its consequences—strokes, heart attacks, kidney failure, senility and loss of limbs. Increasing the amount of fiber in the diet almost automatically decreases the consumption of fat. And the fiber itself lowers blood cholesterol.

Women who are at high risk for breast cancer would do well to follow a cancer-prevention research experiment being conducted by Dr. William DeWys of the National Cancer Institute, Bethesda, Maryland. They would do well to follow the diet outlined for the participants.

We asked Dr. DeWys to discuss his work at the National Cancer Institute:

"One of the important areas that we are looking at is the role of diet as a factor in determining risks for developing cancer, and one of the dietary factors that we think is particularly important is dietary fat. We are giving that particular emphasis in our studies at this time. In the future we will, of course, expand into other areas, but at the present time dietary fat is a major focus of our interest. The evidence associating dietary fat with certain specific types of cancer is really quite strong at this point. For example, the type of cancers that have been associated with high intake of dietary fat include: cancer of the breast, cancer of the colon, cancer of the prostate, cancer of the endometrium (lining of the uterus) and we think if we can reduce the dietary fat intake in the population, we can have a significant impact to reduce the incidence of these cancers. I would say at the present time the evidence is perhaps 99 percent certain of these associations that I have mentioned, and we're in the process of conducting research projects which will at least theoretically bring them up from 99 percent certainty to 100 percent certainty.

"The specific project that I could describe briefly will involve women who are at high risk for breast cancer, and the risk factors that we will use in this study to select women at high risk will include the presence of breast cancer in a first-degree relative; previous biopsies for benign disease of the breast and a late-age first pregnancy—that is, over age 30. We have evidence from other studies that women who have two or more of these risk factors have a significantly increased risk of breast cancer.

"We are then going to ask half of the women in this study to go on a low-fat diet, while the other half are asked to simply continue their usual diet. In the United States the usual diet is comprised of about 40 percent fat expressed in calories. So, 40 percent of the calories in the U.S. diet are derived from fat. In the experimental diet that we'll be studying in this project, we will aim for 20 percent of the calories to be derived from fat. We think this is an achievable goal, but it will be somewhat difficult. Women will have to make significant changes in their food choices and in their usual dietary intake. But we will provide in the course of this study much helpful information to the women, including shopping guides, menus and various kinds of information that will permit them to, on a day-to-day basis, judge how close they're coming to the diet that we would like for them to achieve for this study.

"Now to explain a little bit about the diet—I think it's helpful to think about what are the major sources of fat in the U.S. diet and what strategies can be used to reduce these sources of fat in the diet. The three main categories of foods that are richest in fat include the meats, dairy products and what we call fats and oils. Often people, when they think of fat, think of the fat associated with meat but may not immediately think of the other two categories that I've mentioned. It turns out that the fats and oils category is probably the largest source of fat in the U.S. diet and in many ways is the one that can be adjusted with the least adverse effect on your overall diet. By the fats and oil category we include such things as butter and margarine that are used on sandwiches. We include salad dressings, oils that are used in baking, for example, baking of cakes and pastries. A significant amount of oil is used in the preparation of these foods, and these foods are ones that people can readily give up without losing important nutrients. So, an important recommendation that we would make to the general public in terms of reducing their fat intake will be to avoid or minimize their use of the foods in the fats and oil category. Turning next to the meat category, we have a series of suggestions that would be easily implemented to reduce the fat content drawn from meat. One suggestion is to make food choices in the direction of selecting more fish and poultry and making fewer choices from the red-meat category, the beef and the pork category. Second, we suggest that when people prepare their foods, prior to any cooking they remove all visible fat from beef or pork. And, if they are using poultry they remove the skin, because in poultry much of the fat is associated with the skin. We recommend that the cooking method is important, and the particular method that we recommend involves cooking the meat on a rack so that any fat that is released by the cooking process can drip off from the meat and be discarded, and not eaten with the meat. We particularly discourage the use of frying.

"The reservation that I have about the wok is that the temperature employed there may be higher than advantageous and the temperature at which a food is prepared is another factor that we have some concern about. There is evidence that preparation of foods at very high temperatures will cause the formation of certain chemicals which have been shown to have mutagenic activity. Now, mutagenic activity means that this chemical will damage the DNA, which is the genetic information in a cell, and many chemicals that are mutagenic are also carcinogenic, that is, they can cause cancers. The evidence at this point is incomplete as to whether these chemicals formed by cooking at high temperatures indeed can cause cancer. But, the fact that they are mutagens gives us concern that they also may be carcinogens and could cause cancer. So we recommend cooking foods at moderate temperatures, rather than at very high temperatures.

The other thing to comment about in terms of food choices is that because the fat that is on the outside of a food may be trimmed off, that should not be a particular concern when one is purchasing meat. What one should look at when purchasing meat is the marbling, the fat that is distributed through the meat, because that can't be trimmed off and discarded. So the selection should be based on finding meats with less marbling and that way, less fat would be retained in the meat after the visible fat has been trimmed off.

"One should buy the less marbled, less expensive cuts. Now to a certain extent those cuts may be less flavorful or may be less tender and again, one will have to make some adjustments in cooking to account for that—either cooking for a long period of time in terms of the tender aspect, or using flavor enhancers, or serving the meat with various kinds of added spices. Using the meat in stews, for example, to add spices may be worthwhile consideration.

"There has been a significant trend over the past years toward leaner pork being available. We laud that. That's a very important contribution that the meat industry is making toward the health of the population in this country. We encourage the meat industry to continue that trend and try to increasingly develop strains of animals which will have a lower fat content in the meat. Fortunately, the meat industry is coming to our help in that they are making available low-fat prepared foods—low-fat hams, low-fat luncheon meats—so that one can make selections of recently available products which will be low in fat.

"Unfortunately, we don't have a low-fat hot dog and that is in part because of the rules of the Food & Drug Administration that requires something called the standard of identity. For a food to be called a hot dog, it has to have a certain composition, and until they change the rule we will not have a low-fat hot dog.

"Another area of food choice that is important in terms of reduction of dietary fat is the dairy product area, and here we recommend that people choose either low-fat or non-fat dairy products such as skim milk, low-fat cottage cheese, low-fat yogurt and ice milk in preference to ice cream. These changes in food choice can also contribute to lowering the total fat content in the diet. So these are important to consider also.

"We recommend that people increase their intake of foods from the fruits, vegetables and cereal-grains category. We would suggest that people double or more their current intake in that regard, and specifically the cereal products that should be chosen are whole-grain products. The raisin bran or all bran as a breakfast-cereal choice or whole-grain breads in preference to white bread as sources of grain-related products. I mentioned the fruits and vegetables. These are important as a source of dietary fiber which may be protective for colon cancer. They also are an important source for other nutrients. One of these nutrients which may be important in protecting against cancer is Vitamin A. The Vitamin A category of nutrients and the particular fruits and vegetables which are rich in Vitamin A are those which have a yellow color or a dark green color. So we recommend that people make several choices each day from that broad category—foods such as squash, carrots, tomatoes from the yellow category. For the green category—broccoli, spinach, etc. These will then provide more than adequate intake for Vitamin A in the diet. This will be protective against another category of cancers. The evidence suggests that diets with a high intake of Vitamin A may be protective against lung cancer, cancer of the mouth, larynx and the esophagus."

The typical American diet contains too much fat and can lead to other serious problems, including obesity. High-fat foods are high-caloric foods. Americans spend billions of dollars each year trying to undo what their dietary folly has done to them; prudence shouts for prevention of obesity rather than its treatment.

In nations where the diet has high fiber content, obesity does not occur. The high-fiber foods suggested in this book will help you to avoid unwanted weight gain and even help you to lose some weight.

Dr. James Anderson, of the University of Kentucky in Lexington, has shown that water-soluble fiber has a greater effect on lowering cholesterol than does insoluble fiber. His research has also shown that the soluble fiber lessens the amount of insulin required by maturity-onset diabetics. The insoluble fiber has a greater effect on constipation. For this reason we have included both soluble and insoluble foods in our recipes.

A favorite food for increasing insoluble fiber intake is wheat bran. It is ironic that we have been saving the part of the wheat with less value to our digestion and discarding the more valuable bran. Wheat bran is a source of fiber hard to equal.

Dr. Vincent DeVita, one of the foremost bran advocates we know, reports that he adds bran to his breakfast daily, and when he travels, he locates the restaurants that make good bran muffins. Dr. DeVita feels that eating bran is a good measure for avoiding cancer of the bowel.

Remember! Fiber is filling. The bulk of the fiber foods gives you the sensation of fullness and satisfaction with far fewer calories than you would consume filling up with refined flour breads and simple sugars.

Dr. Denis Burkitt, who spent many years serving the natives of Africa, noted that those who ate high-fiber cereal and vegetable diets were free of most gastrointestinal diseases. These people did not develop gallstones or gall-bladder disease; they did not develop appendicitis, cancer of the bowel, constipation, diverticulitis, hemorrhoids, varicose veins—all common in our culture. It is difficult to overemphasize the importance of fiber in the diet. Increasing the use of fiber is another primary goal of this cookbook because we know that populations who eat only whole-grain and other high-fiber foods are particularly immune to cancer of the colon as well as a whole litany of other ailments.

As we take positive steps toward improving our physical well-being, we are reminded that our "body is a temple of the Holy Spirit" and that we are to "honor God in [our] body" (*see* 1 Corinthians 6: 19, 20 *RSV*).

So here it is: a cookbook with your health in mind, based on principles shown to give you the best chance for avoiding not only cancer but a host of other maladies that plague modern man. At the same time, you will optimize your wellness and allow yourself to enjoy life to its fullest as "God is able to provide you with every blessing in abundance . . . ." (2 Corinthians 9:8 *RSV*).

CORY SERVAAS, M.D.

TO AVOID CANCER

(Evidence for these measures is either overwhelming or very good.)
- Permit no smoking in your home.
- Eat foods high in fiber each day: bran cereals, whole-grain breads, fresh fruits and vegetables.
- Eat foods low in fat.
- If you drink alcoholic beverages, do so only in moderation.
- Avoid unnecessary X-rays.
- Avoid excessive sunlight; use high-number sun screens; cover up.
- If possible, avoid taking estrogens and take only as long as necessary.

Lysine Content in Common Foods

Foods listed with mg. of lysine per 100 grams serving

Food	Mg. of lysine	Food	Mg. of lysine
Apples	22	Fish, fresh	
Apricots	23	Catfish	1590
Asparagus	96	Cod	1703
Avocado	59	Flounder	1631
Beans, dry	1593	Haddock	1703
Beans, lima	1466	Salmon	1604
Beans, mung	1927	Sole	1631
Beef	1573	Snapper	1605
Beets	60	Swordfish	2238
Brewer's yeast, dried	3509	Tuna	2238
Carrots	44	Trout	1604
Cauliflower	160	Whitefish	1604
Cheese	1559	Lamb	1275
Chicken	1590	Milk, cow's	248
Cottage cheese	276	Peaches	30
Crustaceans	1262	Pears	14
Dates	81	Pork	961
Eggplant	222	Potato	96
Eggs	863	Spinach	159
Figs	48	Tomatoes	32
Fish, canned	1844	Turnips	17

Data Source—*Amino-Acid Content of Foods and Biological Data
on Proteins* by the Food Policy and Food Science Service, Nutrition Division.

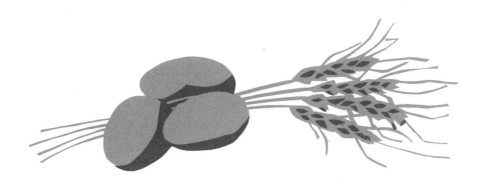

Fiber Content in Common Foods

Quantities listed are the grams of crude fiber
in one 100-gram serving of the edible portion.

	Grams		Grams
Almonds	2.6	Broccoli	1.5
Apples, unpeeled	1.0	Brussels sprouts	1.6
Apples, peeled	.6	Bulgur, cooked	.8
Apricots	.6	Cabbage	.8
Apricots, dried	3.8	Cantaloupe	.3
Artichokes	2.4	Carrots	1.0
Asparagus	.7	Cashew nuts	1.4
Avocado	1.6	Cauliflower	1.0
Banana	.5	Celery	.6
Barley, pearled	.5	Cherries	.1
Beans, dry, cooked	1.5	Chestnuts	1.1
Beans, green or snap	1.0	Chives	1.1
Beans, mung	.7	Coconut	.5
Beets	.8	Collards	1.2
Beet greens	1.1	Corn, sweet	.7
Black-eyed peas	1.8	Corn cereals	
Blackberries	4.1	Flakes	.7
Blueberries	1.5	Puffed	.4
Boysenberries	1.9	Corn bread	.5
Bran (see Wheat bran)		Crackers	
Bran cereals (see		Saltines	.4
Wheat bran cereals)		Graham	1.1
Brazil nuts	3.1	Whole wheat	2.4
Bread		Rye, whole grain	2.2
Boston brown	.7	Cranberries	1.4
Cracked wheat	.5	Cucumbers	.6
Raisin	.9	Currants	2.4
Rye	.4	Dandelion greens	1.3
Pumpernickel	1.1	Dates	2.3
White	.2	Eggplant	.9
Whole wheat	1.6	Elderberries	7.0

	Grams		Grams
Endive (escarole)	.9	Oat cereals	
Farina	.4	Shredded	1.8
Figs, fresh	1.2	Puffed	1.1
Figs, dried	5.6	Flakes (with soy)	.9
Filberts (hazelnuts)	3.0	Oatmeal (rolled oats)	
Gooseberries	1.9	Dry	1.2
Grapefruit	.2	Cooked	.2
Grapes	.6	Okra	1.0
Grits (hominy), cooked	.1	Olives	1.3
Guavas	5.6	Onions, mature	.6
Hickory nuts	1.9	Onions, green	
Kale	1.3	(scallions)	1.0
Kohlrabi	1.0	Oranges	.5
Kumquats	3.7	Orange juice	.1
Leeks	1.3	Parsley	1.4
Lentils, cooked	1.2	Parsnips	2.0
Lettuce	.5	Peaches, fresh	.6
Loganberries	3.0	Peaches, canned	.4
Macadamia nuts	2.5	Peaches, dried	4.0
Macaroni, cooked	.1	Peanuts	2.7
Mangos	.9	Peanut butter	1.9
Millet, cooked	3.2	Pears, unpeeled	1.4
Miso (fermented		Pears, canned	.7
soybeans	2.3	Peas, green	2.0
Muffins, bran	1.8	Peas, dry split, cooked	.4
Muffins, corn	.5	Pecans	2.3
Mushrooms	.8	Peppers, green	1.4
Mustard greens	.9	Persimmons	1.5
Nectarines	.4	Pimiento, canned	.6
Noodles, cooked	.1	Pineapple, fresh	.4

	Grams		Grams
Pineapple, canned	.3	Squash, summer,	.6
Pistachio nuts	1.9	Squash, winter	1.4
Plums	.4	Strawberries	1.3
Pomegranate pulp	.2	Sunflower seeds	3.8
Popcorn	2.2	Sweet potatoes	.9
Potatoes, baked		Swiss chard	.7
in skins	.6	Tangerines	.5
Potatoes, boiled	.4	Tomatoes	.5
Prunes, dried	1.6	Turnips	.9
Prunes, cooked	.8	Waffles, white flour	.1
Pumpkin	1.3	Walnuts, black	1.7
Pumpkin seeds	1.9	Walnuts, English	2.1
Radishes	.7	Watercress	.7
Raisins	.9	Watermelon	.3
Raspberries, black	5.1	Wheat bran,	
Raspberries, red	3.0	unprocessed	9.1
Rhubarb	.7	Wheat bran cereals	
Rice, brown, cooked	.3	All-Bran, Bran Buds	7.8
Rice, white, cooked	.1	40% Bran Flakes	3.6
Rice cereals		Raisin Bran Flakes	3.0
Flakes	.6	Wheat cereals	
Puffed	.6	Hot	.2
Rolls and Buns		Puffed	2.0
White	.1	Shredded	2.3
With raisins	.9	Wheat and barley	
Whole wheat	1.6	flakes	1.8
Rutabagas	1.1	Wheat and malted	
Sesame seeds	2.4	barley granules	1.5
Soybeans, cooked	1.4	Wheat germ	2.5
Soybeans, sprouted	.8	Wild rice	1.0
Spinach	.6	Zucchini	.6

BREADS AND BASICS

It makes sense for this cookbook to begin with recipes for breads, soup stocks and salad dressings, because these are things you need to have ready ahead of time. Here, then, is a varied selection of breads, including muffins, popovers and quickbreads, offering good nutrition as well as intriguing flavors and textures. Baking bread at home can bring immense satisfaction to both the cook and those who eat the products. There is something very reassuring in knowing just what ingredients go into bread and in avoiding all the preservatives and additives that go into most store-bought bread, for which shelf life is so important. There is another benefit: you and your family can enjoy the wonderful aroma with which fresh-baked bread fills your kitchen.

Three-Grain Bread

YIELD: 2 LOAVES

2 packages dry yeast
½ cup lukewarm (115°) water
2 cups low-fat skim milk
1 cup high-lysine cornmeal
4 tablespoons corn oil margarine

2 teaspoons sea salt (optional)
2 cups triticale flour
2 cups whole wheat pastry flour
2 cups unbleached flour
4 tablespoons honey

Combine the yeast and water, stirring until smooth. Cover and let stand 5 minutes.

Scald the milk. Gradually add the cornmeal, stirring constantly with a wooden spoon. When the mixture is well blended, stir in the margarine, honey and salt (if desired). Set aside to cool to lukewarm.

Combine the cornmeal mixture and yeast in an electric mixing bowl. Add the triticale and whole wheat flours, and knead 8 minutes with the dough hook or 10 minutes by hand.

Grease a bowl lightly with margarine and put in the dough, turning it around so that it is lightly coated on all sides. Cover and let rise for 1½ hours or until doubled.

Grease or vegetable-spray two 9¼-inch by 5¼-inch bread pans. Punch down the bread and divide it in half. Shape into loaves and place in the pans. Cover and let rise until doubled.

Preheat the oven to 425° F. Bake the bread 25 minutes. Turn out immediately onto racks to cool.

Hi-Ly Peasant Bread

1 package dry yeast
½ cup lukewarm (115°) water
1 cup evaporated skim milk
2 tablespoons brown sugar
2 teaspoons salt (optional)

2 tablespoons corn oil margarine
1¼ cups whole wheat pastry flour
1½ cups all-purpose unbleached
   flour
½ cup high-lysine cornmeal

Dissolve the yeast in the water with 1 teaspoon of brown sugar. Cover and let stand while preparing the rest of the recipe.

Heat the milk with the remaining sugar, the salt, if desired and the margarine, stirring until margarine dissolves. Cool to lukewarm and mix with the yeast and the whole wheat flour and 1 cup of the unbleached flour. Beat with a dough hook for 5 minutes. Cover and let rise for as long as it takes to double in volume.

Add the cornmeal and enough more unbleached flour to make a firm dough. Knead for 5 minutes. Turn into a well greased bowl. Cover and let rise in a warm place until doubled.

Grease or vegetable-spray a 9-inch layer cake pan. Turn the dough onto a lightly floured surface and knead into a round loaf. Place in the sun and let rise until doubled.

Preheat the oven to 400° F. Bake the bread for 10 minutes. Reduce the temperature to 350° F. and continue baking for 35 minutes. Remove from the pan to a rack to cool.

Hi-Fiber Sally Lunn
YIELD: 2 LOAVES

1 cup low-fat or skim milk
1 stick corn oil margarine
2 cups triticale flour, sifted
5 tablespoons sugar
1½ teaspoons salt (optional)

2 cups all-purpose unbleached
  flour
2 packages dry yeast
3 large eggs

Butter or vegetable-spray 2 loaf pans. Heat the margarine and milk until very warm to the touch (120° F.)

Combine ½ cup of triticale flour and ½ cup of the flour with the sugar and salt, if desired and the yeast in a mixing bowl. Beat in the very warm liquid, beating constantly, and continue to beat for 2 minutes. Gradually add ½ cup more of the triticale flour and the eggs and beat hard for 2 minutes longer. Gradually add the remaining flour until you have a dough that is thick but not stiff. Cover and let rise for 1½ hours or until doubled in bulk.

Punch down the dough and divide in half. Shape into 2 loaves and place in the prepared pans. Cover with a dish towel and let rise until it has increased by one half. Preheat the oven to 350° F. and bake 45 minutes.

Quick Triticale Corn Bread

YIELD: 1 LOAF

1 cup high-lysine cornmeal
1 cup triticale flour
1 cup sifted unbleached
  all-purpose flour
4 tablespoons brown sugar

5 teaspoons baking powder
3 large eggs
1½ cups low-fat or skim milk
5 tablespoons corn-oil margarine,
  melted

Preheat the oven to 400° F. Grease or vegetable-spray a 9¼-inch by 5¼-inch bread pan.

    Combine the dry ingredients in one bowl. In another bowl beat the eggs and milk together for 1 minute. Add the melted margarine.

    Combine the mixtures, stirring as briefly as possible. Pour into the prepared pan and bake for 25 minutes.

Triticale Cheddar Bread

YIELD: 1 LOAF

Fast-rising yeast is good to use with triticale flour, which tends to be a little heavier than the other flours we're accustomed to. Allow extra time for the dough to rise if you use ordinary yeast.

1 tablespoon fast-rising dry yeast
½ cup warm (115°) water
2 cups unbleached all-purpose flour
1 teaspoon sea salt (optional)

2½ tablespoons dry skim milk
¾ cup warm water
1½ cups triticale flour
1 cup cheddar cheese, diced

Dissolve the yeast in the warm water in a large warmed mixing bowl. Cover and let stand 15 minutes.

    Stir in ½ cup of unbleached flour. Cover and let stand 30 minutes.

    Dissolve the sea salt and skim milk powder in the ¾ cup of warm water and stir into the yeast mixture. Beat constantly, gradually adding the triticale flour and then the unbleached flour until you have a firm but not stiff dough. Knead 8 minutes with a dough hook or 10 minutes by hand.

    Cover and let rise 30 to 40 minutes (longer if using regular yeast).

    Punch down and incorporate the diced cheese. Knead and form into a loaf. Place in a 9-inch loaf tin that has been greased or vegetable-sprayed. Bake 10 minutes in a preheated 425° F. oven. Reduce the heat to 350° and bake 25 minutes longer. Turn out immediately onto a rack to cool.

Hi-Ly Cheese Corn Bread

1 cup high-lysine cornmeal
1½ teaspoons baking powder
⅛ teaspoon white pepper
½ teaspoon salt (optional)
2 eggs
1 stick corn oil margarine, melted

1 cup plain yogurt
4 ounces sharp cheddar cheese, grated
1 package (10 ounces) frozen corn kernels, slightly thawed

Preheat the oven to 375° F. Butter or vegetable-spray a 12-inch by 8-inch pan.
Spin the cornmeal in a food processor. Add the remaining dry ingredients.
Beat the eggs in a bowl for 1 minute. Add the melted margarine and yogurt. Add the dry ingredients and stir until well blended. Stir in the corn kernels.
Pour half the batter into the pan, spreading it evenly with a spatula. Sprinkle with the grated cheese and pour the remaining batter over all.
Bake 30 to 35 minutes. Cut in squares to serve.

Old-Fashioned Johnny Cake and Herbed Corn Bread Stuffing Mix

Two recipes in one

If you are going to make corn bread for breakfast or brunch, it is a good time to make the Herbed Corn Bread Stuffing Mix which you can store in the freezer until such time that you plan to stuff Cornish Hens, a chicken or even a small turkey.

1½ cups high-lysine cornmeal
2 cups unbleached all-purpose flour
4 tablespoons sugar
2 tablespoons baking powder
½ teaspoon salt (optional)
1 cup yogurt
1 cup milk
2 large eggs, well beaten

3 tablespoons corn oil margarine melted
Herbs:
4 tablespoons onion, minced, sauteed
1½ tablespoons sage leaves, crumbled
3 tablespoons parsley, chopped

Preheat the oven to 400° F. Grease or vegetable-spray 2 9¼-inch by 5¼-inch pans. Prepare the onion and herbs. Mix the dry ingredients together.
Combine the yogurt; milk and beaten eggs. When well mixed, add the margarine. Mix the liquids with the dry ingredients just until blended. Pour half the batter into one of the greased pans.

Mix the herbs with the remaining batter and pour into the second pan. Bake 20 to 25 minutes or until golden brown.

Let the Herbed Corn Bread stand at room temperature for 24 hours or until it is stale and crumbly. Break into crumbs with your fingers and store in freezer bags.

Hi-Ly Popovers

YIELD: 12 POPOVERS

½ cup high-lysine cornmeal (plain or pulverized)
½ cup unbleached all-purpose flour

½ teaspoon salt (optional)
3 large eggs
1 cup low-fat milk
1 tablespoon corn oil

Preheat the oven to 400° F. Grease or vegetable-spray 12 muffin tins or custard cups. Mix the cornmeal, flour and salt.

Beat the eggs until light. Stir in the dry ingredients, then add the milk and corn oil. Beat hard for 3 minutes.

Pour the tins half full. Bake 35 minutes. Prick with a fork and continue to bake 5 minutes.

Savoury Hi-Ly Triticale Muffins

YIELD: 12-3 INCH MUFFINS

1 cup high-lysine cornmeal, pulverized
1 cup triticale flour
½ cup unbleached all-purpose flour
½ teaspoon salt (optional)
2 tablespoons brown sugar
2 tablespoons corn oil margarine, melted

6 teaspoons baking powder
3 teaspoons onion, minced
2 teaspoons green pepper, minced
2 teaspoons pimiento, minced
½ teaspoon powdered sage
2 eggs, beaten until light
1 cup low-fat milk

Preheat the oven to 400° F. Grease or vegetable-spray muffin tins.

Mix all the dry ingredients in a bowl.

Prepare the vegetables. Add them and the sage to the beaten eggs, milk and margarine and stir until blended. Pour into the dry ingredients and mix them briefly but thoroughly.

Half fill the prepared pan and bake 20 minutes. Serve with cottage cheese.

Hy-Ly Mashed Potato Muffins

YIELD: 12 MUFFINS

2 or 3 potatoes
2 tablespoons corn oil margarine
1 tablespoon honey
1 teaspoon sea salt (optional)

1 cup high-lysine cornmeal
4 tablespoons powdered skim milk
1 tablespoon baking powder
1 egg, well beaten

Vegetable-spray a large muffin pan. Peel the potatoes, cut them in squares and boil, covered, in 1½ cups of lightly salted water until tender. Drain, reserving the liquid. Boil down the water until it measures ¾ cup.

Meanwhile, mash the potatoes. You should have 1 cup full. Combine the potato with the margarine, honey and salt (if desired), and the potato water. Stir well and cool to lukewarm.

Preheat the oven to 400°F. Mix the cornmeal, skim milk powder and baking powder and stir in the potato mixture just until blended. Add the egg and mix thoroughly.

Fill medium size muffin pans two-thirds full. Bake 20 to 25 minutes or until golden brown.

Scotch Bannock

YIELD: 4 to 6 SERVINGS

A bannock is a large scone, cooked in one circle and cut into wedges. If the cornmeal is pulverized before mixing it has a slightly lighter texture, but the coarser meal gives it a chewy texture that seems delightfully rugged and Scottish.

1 cup high-lysine cornmeal
  (plain or pulverized)
1 cup oatmeal flakes
1 cup buttermilk

½ teaspoon salt (optional)
2 tablespoons corn oil
2 tablespoons brown sugar
1 teaspoon baking soda

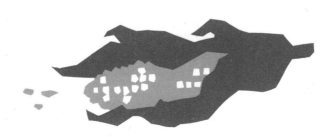

Preheat the oven to 375° F. Heat a 9-inch frying pan or oven-proof nonstick skillet with 1 tablespoon of corn oil.

Combine all the ingredients in a mixing bowl and when the skillet is hot, pour the mixture into the skillet. Cook 10 minutes over moderately high heat.

Transfer to the oven and bake 20 minutes. Remove from the oven and cut in wedges. Serve with unsalted butter or margarine and bitter orange marmalade.

Carrot Raisin Bread

YIELD: 1 LOAF

¾ cup corn oil
1 cup honey
1 cup triticale or whole wheat
   pastry flour
½ cup unbleached flour, sifted
1 teaspoon baking powder
1 teaspoon soda

¼ teaspoon ground cloves
1 teaspoon cinnamon
½ teaspoon salt (optional)
1 teaspoon vanilla extract
1 cup raw carrots, grated
1 cup golden raisins
2 large eggs

Preheat the oven to 350° F. Grease or vegetable-spray an 8-inch loaf tin. Stir the oil and honey together.

Combine the triticale and unbleached flour with the baking powder, soda, cloves, cinnamon and salt, if desired. Stir into the oil mixture. Add the vanilla, carrots and raisins and, when blended, add the eggs one by one, beating hard after each addition. Pour into the prepared pan and bake 50 minutes. Turn onto a rack to cool.

Hi-Ly Whole Wheat Cinnamon Rolls

YIELD: 35 ROLLS

2 cups low-fat milk
3 tablespoons corn oil margarine
2 tablespoons sugar
½ teaspoon salt (optional)
2 cups high-lysine cornmeal
2½ cups whole wheat pastry flour
2½ cups unbleached all-purpose
   flour

2 packages dry yeast
¼ cup lukewarm (115°) water
2 whole eggs (room temperature)
Corn oil margarine (for spreading)
½ cup brown sugar
1 tablespoon cinnamon

Scald the milk and remove from the heat. Stir in the 3 tablespoons of margarine, the sugar and the salt, if desired. Cool to lukewarm.

Pulverize the cornmeal in a blender and combine in a bowl with the other flours. Dissolve the yeast in the lukewarm water and mix with the milk in an electric mixing bowl. Beat in half the flour and when well blended, add the eggs. Continue beating until well mixed.

Add the remaining flour gradually until you have a fairly stiff, though still soft dough. Knead with a dough hook for 8 minutes or by hand for 10 minutes. The dough should be smooth and elastic. Add more unbleached flour if necessary. Cover with a double thickness of toweling and let rise at room temperature until doubled and light.

Punch down and place in a vegetable-sprayed bowl. Cover and keep in the refrigerator overnight.

The next morning, knead the dough down to remove any air pockets and cut the dough in half for easier handling. Roll each half out to a rectangle approximately 18 inches by 10 inches and ¾ inch thick. Spread lightly with margarine and sprinkle with half the brown sugar and half the cinnamon. Roll up like a jelly roll and cut in 1-inch slices. Place close together in a buttered 14-inch by 18-inch roasting pan. Cover and let rise until doubled— approximately 50 minutes.

Preheat the oven to 450° F. and bake the rolls 15 minutes.

For special occasions, spread the rolls with some confectioners' sugar mixed smooth with milk to give a spreading consistency.

Chicken Stock

No self-respecting kitchen should ever be without a good supply of chicken stock. The homemade variety is the best because the canned chicken broths are usually loaded with salt for better preservation. A good supply of chicken stock placed in several different sizes of containers is the best culinary insurance possible. This recipe can be doubled or tripled.

2 pounds chicken carcass
   (bones, wings, neck, trimmings)
1 clove garlic
1 large carrot
1 large onion

1 stalk celery
1 sprig thyme
1 bay leaf
3 sprigs parsley
1 teaspoon salt (optional)

Chop the carcass roughly. Crush the garlic clove with the side of a knife blade. Do not bother to peel. Prepare the vegetables and cut into large pieces. Put everything in a soup kettle. Add the herbs and 3 quarts of water. Salt can be added if desired.

Bring to a boil over moderate heat, skimming off any froth that rises to the surface. Simmer 2 hours. Skim once more. Cool and strain through a fine strainer. Chill to let the fat rise to the top. Skim the fat off and discard. Pour the broth into containers and store in the refrigerator or freezer.

Vegetable Broth

No exact recipe can be given for this useful ingredient. Vegetable stock or broth is the liquid the wise cook saves when cooking vegetables and stores in a covered jar in the refrigerator. Additional stock can be made from vegetable trimmings—pea pods, carrot skins, bean ends, parsley stems and onion tops—cooked in water enough to cover them. Simmer for 30 minutes, then strain and store in the refrigerator. Use vegetable broth to add both flavor and nutrition when making soups and sauces.

SALAD DRESSINGS
Cottage Cheese Dressing

1 tablespoon shallots, minced	1 cup low-fat cottage cheese
4 tablespoons chili sauce	½ cup yogurt
4 tablespoons tarragon wine vinegar	2 tablespoons mayonnaise
½ teaspoon salt (optional)	

Put everything in a food processor and spin 30 seconds. Transfer to a bowl. Cover and chill for an hour before using.

Herb Vinaigrette
YIELD: 1½ CUPS

⅓ cup red wine vinegar
⅔ cup safflower oil
⅓ cup olive oil
½ teaspoon basil, chopped
3 teaspoons parsley, chopped

1 clove garlic, minced (optional)
2 teaspoons soy sauce
¼ teaspoon black pepper, freshly ground
⅛ teaspoon Tabasco

Combine all the ingredients and let the flavors meld for several hours.

Processor Mayonnaise
YIELD: 1½ CUPS

2 eggs
2 tablespoons white wine vinegar or lemon juice
1 teaspoon dry mustard
½ teaspoon salt (optional)

⅛ teaspoon white pepper
⅔ cup oil (safflower or corn)
⅓ cup olive oil
⅛ teaspoon Tabasco (optional)
2 tablespoons boiling water

Combine the eggs, vinegar, seasonings and 4 tablespoons of oil in a food processor or blender. Spin at high speed for 5 seconds. Start adding the remaining oil in a very fine stream through the tube.

When all the oil is absorbed, add the Tabasco, if desired, and pour in the boiling water slowly. This will make the mayonnaise less oily and it will keep much longer under refrigeration.

Yogurt Fruit Salad Dressing

4 tablespoons fresh orange juice
1 tablespoon fresh lemon juice
2 tablespoons honey
1 cup plain yogurt

2 tablespoons chives, chopped
¼ teaspoon salt (optional)
¼ teaspoon white pepper

Stir all the ingredients in a bowl until blended. Cover and chill.

BREAKFASTS

Breakfast is a very important meal, too often neglected. It has been proven countless times that people with sustaining and healthy breakfasts work better, study harder and produce much more than those who settle for a quick cup of coffee on the way out the door. If properly planned, breakfast can fulfill a large percentage of the day's fiber and nutritional requirements, and all very pleasantly. Brunch, an American invention, is a more substantial and varied meal served at a later hour, for guests. The menus suggested here are for an informal occasion, where the hostess (or host) prepares the entree after the guests assemble. This preparation can take place at a buffet or side table in the dining room, or even on porch or patio, if the proper appliances are available.

Hi-Fiber Cereal Sundae

There is no recipe for this concoction because it is up to the provider to arrange three or four different kinds of high fiber cereals in a bowl as fancy dictates and to sprinkle it with raisins, or chopped dates or fresh fruit. A dash of cinnamon to spice it up can be included. A pitcher of milk will be on the table.

Avocado Toasts

YIELD: 4 SERVINGS

1 large avocado
1 large clove garlic
1 teaspoon lemon juice
⅛ teaspoon Tabasco sauce

⅛ teaspoon salt (optional)
4 cherry tomatoes
4 slices Three Grain Bread

Peel, seed and mash the avocado with a fork. Press the garlic and add it to the avocado. Add the lemon juice, Tabasco and salt, if desired. Work together well. Cut the cherry tomatoes in 4 wedges each.

Just before serving, toast the bread from which the crusts have been removed. Spread evenly with the avocado. Garnish each corner with a wedge of tomato.

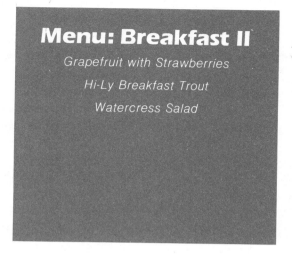

Grapefruit with Strawberries

YIELD: 4 SERVINGS

2 large grapefruit
1 pint strawberries

2 teaspoons honey
(optional)

Cut the grapefruit in half. Remove the center cores and loosen the individual sections with a grapefruit knife.

Wash the strawberries very briefly. Pick out the 4 prettiest berries and save with their leaves on. Hull the rest and force them through a food mill or strainer.

Stir in the honey, if desired, and when it has dissolved pour the mixture over the grapefruit and let it seep through. Chill the grapefruit. Just before serving garnish the centers with the whole strawberries.

Hi-Ly Breakfast Trout

YIELD: 4 SERVINGS

4 whole 8-ounce trout (fresh
   or frozen)
½ cup high-lysine cornmeal
   (pulverized)
½ teaspoon salt (optional)

½ teaspoon white pepper
⅛ teaspoon paprika
Safflower oil
4 tablespoons corn oil margarine
Lemon wedges and parsley

Advance preparation: The night before wash the trout (thaw if frozen), and shake off all excess moisture. Dip into a mixture of the cornmeal and seasonings dusting both inside and out. Place on a platter. Cover with wax paper and refrigerate.

Shortly before serving, heat the oil in a large skillet to 360° F. or until sizzling hot. Fry the trout on both sides allowing 4 minutes to each side. If the temperature of the oil is hot enough very little of the oil will be absorbed. Drain on toweling.

Transfer each trout to an individual heated plate. Pour over 2 teaspoons of the hot margarine. Garnish with a wedge of lemon and a sprig of parsley.

Watercress Salad

YIELD: 4 SERVINGS

1 large bunch watercress
1 fresh cucumber, seeded and diced
3 tablespoons red wine vinegar
¾ cup low fat cottage cheese

2 tablespoons corn oil
1 tablespoon chives, chopped
1 tablespoon parsley, chopped
½ teaspoon salt (optional)

Pick over the watercress, removing any yellow leaves and breaking off all but the very tender stems. Wash and chill in the refrigerator.

Peel, seed and dice the cucumber. Stir the vinegar, cottage cheese and oil until well blended. Stir in the diced cucumber, the chives and parsley. Add salt if desired.

To serve, put ¼ cup of the cucumber mixture in the bottom of individual salad bowls or plates. Top with the cold watercress leaves.

Menu: Breakfast III

*Fresh Papaya Halves with
Blueberries*

*Kippered Herring with Broiled
Tomatoes*

*Toasted Three Grain Bread
(see Breads and Basics)*

Corn Oil Margarine and Marmalade

Fresh Papaya Halves with Blueberries

Papayas are sold in supermarkets all over the country now. They are delicious as well as marvelously nutritious. To be fully ripe they should be orange-skinned although they are usually sold green. So plan ahead.

To serve them, split in half and remove the seeds. Fill the center with blueberries. The papaya is so sweet that no sugar is necessary.

Kippered Herring with Broiled Tomatoes

YIELD: 4 SERVINGS

4 large canned kippered herring
1 tablespoon melted corn oil
margarine
8 large cherry tomatoes
2 tablespoons fine bread crumbs

Oregano, parsley
1 tablespoon corn oil
Lemon juice
Black Pepper

Place the herring in a single layer in the center of an ovenproof serving dish. Sprinkle with freshly ground black pepper and paint with melted margarine.

Halve the tomatoes and place them around the herring. Sprinkle each one with the breadcrumbs which have been mixed with a little oregano. Brush with oil.

Brown under the broiler for 5 minutes or until thoroughly heated and lightly browned. Sprinkle the herring with a little lemon juice and garnish with chopped parsley.

Menu: Brunch

Orange Mint Julep

One Egg Omelets with Fillings:
Shrimp Creole
Raw Mushroom
Herbed Chicken Cream
Strawberry Applesauce

New England Corn Bread Fritters
Maple Syrup

Hi-Ly Whole Wheat Cinnamon Rolls
(see Breads and Basics)

Orange Mint Julep

YIELD: 4 SERVINGS

2 tablespoons minced mint
2 tablespoons sugar
1 quart freshly squeezed orange juice

1 cup lemon sherbet
Mint leaves

Chill 4 tall glasses in the freezer.

Work the mint and sugar together with the back of a spoon until thoroughly blended. Divide between the glasses.

Spin the orange juice and the sherbet in a blender and pour into the glasses. Garnish each glass with mint leaves and serve with straws.

One Egg Omelets

One egg omelets make an excellent brunch or lunch dish. With a good filling, one omelet makes a satisfying serving, and for those who want more than one filling, a second omelet is quickly made. The omelets should always be made on demand and the fillings should be "ready to go."

I scant teaspoon corn oil
   margarine
1 egg

2 teaspoons water
⅛ teaspoon salt (optional)
Pinch of pepper

Heat the margarine in a small non-stick skillet. Beat the egg, water and seasonings with a small whisk or a fork, just until blended. Pour the mixture into the hot fat and let the egg coagulate on the bottom, stirring gently with a wooden spatula. As the egg cooks, lift up the edges to let the uncooked liquid slip underneath. While the top side is still a little runny, add a large spoonful of the desired filling. Fold one half over the other and turn upside down onto a warm plate. This is a very quick operation.

Shrimp Creole Omelet Filling

Make this in advance and reheat *without* boiling just before serving. Serve in a heatproof dish and keep warm on a hot tray. It's always better the second day.

3 tablespoons corn oil margarine
2 tablespoons whole wheat
   pastry flour
1 medium large onion, chopped
1 medium green pepper, chopped
1 clove garlic, minced

2 tablespoons tomato paste
½ pound cooked shrimp
1½ cups chicken stock
⅛ teaspoon Tabasco
½ teaspoon salt (optional)

Heat the margarine and stir in the flour. Stir over moderate heat until the mixture is well browned, but do not scorch.

Add the chopped vegetables and cook until the onion is soft, stirring frequently. Stir in the tomato paste and the chicken stock. Cook until thickened slightly. Add the seasonings and finally the shrimp. Heat, but do not let the sauce boil.

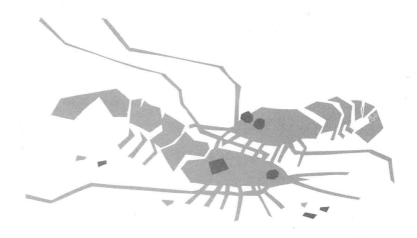

Raw Mushroom Omelet Filling

½ pound raw white mushrooms
½ cup scallions, chopped
2 tablespoons Italian parsley,
  chopped

1 pound low-fat cottage cheese
2 teaspoons soy sauce
¼ teaspoon white pepper

Trim the stems of the mushrooms and wash them very briefly. Dry them well and chop them coarsely.

Trim the scallions and chop both the green and white parts. Chop the parsley.

Mix the vegetables with the cottage cheese and soy sauce. Add the pepper and let the mixture stand at least an hour to blend the flavors.

Herbed Chicken Cream Omelet Filling

This can be made in advance and reheated.

4 tablespoons corn oil margarine
2 tablespoons shallots, chopped
4 tablespoons whole wheat pastry
  flour
2¼ cups chicken broth
2 tablespoons skim milk powder

1 teaspoon tarragon, chopped
1 tablespoon parsley, chopped
1 teaspoon lemon juice
2 cups cooked chicken, diced
Salt and pepper (optional)

Heat the margarine and add the shallots. Cook until the shallots are soft. Stir in the flour and continue to stir for 2 minutes.

Add the broth combined with the milk powder and stir until smooth. Add the chopped herbs and the lemon juice. Add the diced chicken and bring to a simmer. Season as desired.

Strawberry Applesauce Omelet Filling

YIELD: 4 SERVINGS

3 MacIntosh apples
3 Granny Smith apples

1 cup fresh strawberries
¾ teaspoon cinnamon

Wash and peel the apples. Divide them into quarters and remove the cores.

Cook the MacIntosh apples in very little water until soft. Mash them to a pulp.

Meanwhile, cut the Granny Smith apples into small chunks. Add the chunks to the pulped apple and bring to a boil. Cook for 5 minutes.

Wash, hull and halve the strawberries. Add berries and the cinnamon to the apples, bring to a boil and cook for 2 minutes. Remove from the stove and cool. Taste for seasoning. Add a little sugar only if necessary.

Serve at room temperature.

New England Corn Bread Fritters

YIELD: 4 SERVINGS

Corn oil
1 cup high-lysine cornmeal (plain or pulverized)
1 cup whole wheat pastry flour
2 teaspoons baking powder

¼ teaspoon salt (optional)
1 cup corn kernels (fresh or frozen)
1 egg
1 cup low-fat milk

Heat corn oil in a deep frying kettle or heat 2 to 3 inches of oil in an electric frying pan.

Mix the dry ingredients in a bowl. Add the corn kernels. Beat the egg and milk until well blended. Stir into the bowl, stirring just long enough to mix everything well.

Drop from the side of a small serving spoon into the hot (375° F. fat, frying 5 or 6 at a time. Turn them as they float to the top. Fry until nicely browned and drain on paper toweling. Serve hot with maple syrup.

LUNCHEONS

Herbs are magic ingredients that can add flavor without adding sodium or cholesterol. You will find basil, tarragon, dill, fennel, cumin and thyme in these recipes for luncheon dishes. Nutritionists tell us that we must include some fiber in every meal and now we know that ideally that means using high-lysine cornmeal and triticale flour. If meals are relatively low calorie as we have planned in these pages, the inclusion of a delicious chewy bread is acceptable for most diets. If you learn to eat bread as the French do—without butter—the calorie count is even lower.

Chicken Waldorf Salad

YIELD: 4 SERVINGS

1 cup chicken meat, diced
¾ cup celery, diced
¾ cup apples, diced (with skins)
3 tablespoons parsley, chopped
2 tablespoons scallions, chopped
1 teaspoon basil, minced

1 teaspoon tarragon, minced
6 tablespoons water chestnuts,
 sliced, lightly toasted
Cottage Cheese Dressing
 (see Breads and Basics)
Tomato wedges

Combine the chicken, celery, apples, parsley, scallions, herbs and water chestnuts. Toss until well blended.

Pack tightly into a vegetable-oil sprayed 4-cup bowl or decorative mold. Chill in the refrigerator for 2 to 3 hours.

Before serving, unmold on a platter lined with lettuce leaves. Spoon the dressing around the base of the mound and garnish with small tomato wedges.

Orange Strawberry Mold

YIELD: 6 to 8 SERVINGS

1 cup orange juice
2 teaspoons lemon juice
1 pint strawberries
1 pint low-fat cottage cheese,
  well drained
3 tablespoons light honey

½ cup diced pineapple
  well drained
1 teaspoon vanilla
1 small can mandarin orange
  sections

Stir together the orange and lemon juice.

Reserve 6 or 8 perfect strawberries for garnish. Wash and hull the remaining berries. Place them in the food processor along with the orange juice, cottage cheese, honey, pineapple and vanilla, and spin until smooth.

Transfer the mixture to a 6-cup ring mold and chill in the refrigerator for at least 3 hours before serving.

Garnish with the reserved berries and the mandarin orange segments, alternating them around the mold.

Menu: Luncheon II

Crab and Rice Stuffed Tomatoes

Hi-Ly Popovers
(see Breads and Basics)

Asparagus on Triticale Cheese Toast

Pineapple Wedges with
Raspberry Sauce

Crab and Rice Stuffed Tomatoes

YIELD: 4 SERVINGS

½ pound crab meat
1 cup cooked brown rice
1 tablespoon chives, chopped
2 tablespoons celery, diced
1 tablespoon parsley, chopped

½ cup Herb Vinaigrette
   (see Breads and Basics)
4 large tomatoes
3 tablespoons mayonnaise
Lettuce leaves

Pick over the crab meat to be sure there are no filaments. Save out all the nice pieces of claw meat. Combine the crab meat with the cooked rice, chives, celery and parsley, and toss with the Vinaigrette. Cover and let stand 30 minutes.

Choose tomatoes of approximately the same size and shape. Scoop out the centers, removing all the seeds and excess liquid. Turn upside down on a rack to drain.

Stir in just enough mayonnaise to bind the stuffing. Season to taste with white pepper and salt, if desired.

Mound the stuffing into the tomatoes, smoothing the top into an inverted cone. Place the claw meat around the sides of the cone and put a sprig of parsley on the top.

Serve on individual salad plates, placing each tomato on a lettuce leaf. Serve with extra Vinaigrette.

Asparagus on Triticale Cheese Toast

YIELD: 4 SERVINGS

20 spears medium size asparagus
4 slices Triticale Cheese Bread
  (see Breads and Basics)
4 tablespoons corn oil margarine

4 tablespoons Parmesan cheese,
  freshly grated
Black pepper, freshly ground

Wash the asparagus and cut off the tough ends. The stems can be peeled with a potato peeler, if desired. Bring 2 inches of water to a boil in a shallow heavy pan. Add the asparagus and cover tightly. Cook 10 minutes or just until tender. Do not overcook. Drain well.

Toast the bread very lightly and place on individual salad plates. Top each slice with 5 spears of asparagus. Pour a tablespoon of melted margarine over each serving and sprinkle with Parmesan and black pepper.

Pineapple Wedges with Raspberry Sauce

YIELD: 4 SERVINGS

1 small very fresh pineapple
1 box (10 ounces) frozen
  raspberries, thawed

4 tablespoons light honey
2 tablespoons frozen orange
  concentrate, thawed

Cut off the top and bottom of the pineapple. Using a very sharp knife, shave off the sides and the eyes, leaving a clean smooth surface. Cut into 4 wedges and remove the hard core. Cover and keep in a cool (not cold) place. Over-chilled fruit has less flavor.

Press the raspberries through a sieve, to remove the seeds. Stir in the honey and orange concentrate. Cover and chill.

To serve: Place the wedges on individual dessert plates. Stir the sauce well and pour some over each wedge.

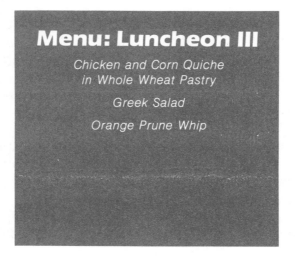

Menu: Luncheon III

*Chicken and Corn Quiche
in Whole Wheat Pastry*

Greek Salad

Orange Prune Whip

Chicken and Corn Quiche
in Whole Wheat Pastry

Pastry:
1 cup whole wheat pastry flour
1 stick cold corn oil margarine
¼ teaspoon salt (optional)
6 tablespoons ice water

Quiche:
1 cup diced chicken

1 cup scraped fresh corn
1 cup low-sodium cheese, grated
⅓ cup scallions, minced
3 large eggs
½ teaspoon hickory smoked salt
**¼ teaspoon black pepper, freshly
   ground**
¾ cup Half and Half® cream

Place the pastry flour in a food processor. Cut up the margarine into 8 pieces and add with the salt to the flour. Spin 10 seconds or until mealy in texture. Add the ice water and spin just until it begins to form a ball.

Remove the ball to a piece of wax paper. Shape with your hands into a ball. Cover and let rest 20 to 30 minutes before rolling out and lining a 9-inch tart pan. Chill in the freezer for 10 minutes while preparing the filling.

Preheat the oven to 425° F. Prepare the chicken, corn, cheese and scallions. Beat the eggs, Half and Half® salt and black pepper together until light.

Distribute the chicken, corn and cheese in the pastry shell. Pour the egg mixture over all and sprinkle with the minced scallions. Bake 10 minutes in the lower third of the oven. Reduce the temperature to 350° F. and bake 40 minutes longer. Let stand 5 to 10 minutes before serving.

Greek Salad

YIELD: SERVINGS

4 artichoke hearts, halved
½ cup fresh fennel, chopped
½ cup Greek olives, sliced
1 tablespoon fresh dill
½ cup scallions, chopped
3 tablespoons red wine vinegar

2 tablespoons olive oil
(preferably Greek)
Salt (optional)
Black pepper, freshly ground
1 head garden lettuce

Combine the artichoke halves (frozen or canned) with the fennel, olives, dill, and scallions in a non-metal bowl. Mix the wine vinegar, oil, salt, (if desired), and pepper. When well blended, pour over the vegetables. Stir well and marinate 2 hours.

To serve: Toss with carefully washed lettuce leaves.

Orange Prune Whip

YIELD: 4 TO 6 SERVINGS

8 ounces sun dried pitted prunes
1 tablespoon frozen orange
concentrate, thawed

2 tablespoons frozen lemonade
concentrate, thawed
3 egg whites
⅛ teaspoon cream of tartar

Cover the prunes with cold water. Bring to a boil and simmer for 20 minutes or until soft. Cool in the remaining liquid.

Spin in a food processor. The result should be 1 cup of thick dark paste. Boil down if too liquid and cool again.

Combine the orange and lemonade concentrates. Beat the egg whites and, when frothy, add the cream of tartar. Beat until stiff but not dry. Fold into the prune mixture and pour into an unbuttered souffle dish (4- cup size).

Place in a pan of hot water and bake 40 minutes at 300° F. Serve plain or with whipped cream.

Hi-Ly Crunchy Corn Spoon Bread

YIELD: 4 SERVINGS

1 cup milk

¾ cup water

¾ cup high-lysine cornmeal

½ teaspoon salt (optional)

½ teaspoon corn oil margarine

3 eggs

2 teaspoons baking powder

⅔ cup corn kernels (fresh or frozen)

Preheat the oven to 350° F. Grease or vegetable spray a small baking dish.

Heat the milk and water in a saucepan. When it starts to simmer, gradually add the cornmeal mixed with the salt (if desired), and whisk until the mixture thickens. Remove from the heat and stir in the margarine.

Beat the eggs until very light. Stir into the cornmeal the eggs, the baking powder and the corn kernels. Pour into the prepared dish and bake 40 minutes.

Serve with unsalted margarine or with Shrimp Creole (see Breakfasts—Shrimp Creole Omelet Filling).

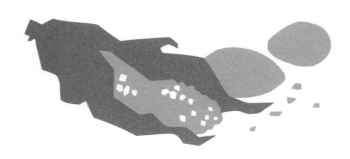

Snow Pea and Tomato Salad

YIELD: 4 SERVINGS

1 pound young snow peas
½ pint cherry tomatoes

2 tablespoons chives, minced
Herb Viniagrette (see Breads
and Basics)

Remove the ends from the snow peas. Throw them into a large kettle of boiling water. Bring them to a boil and cook ½ minute. Drain and put into a pan of very cold water to freshen. Drain and dry.

Wash and halve the tomatoes. Arrange the snow peas spoke-like in a very shallow round platter. Mound the tomatoes in the center and sprinkle with chopped chives.

Toss at the table with ½ cup of Vinaigrette.

Whole Wheat Crepes

Crepes:
½ cup whole wheat pastry flour
1 tablespoon sugar
¼ teaspoon salt (optional)
1 egg
⅔ cup low-fat milk
½ teaspoon vanilla extract

Filling:
8 sun-dried apricots
½ cup honey
1 teaspoon unsalted butter
1 teaspoon orange rind, grated
3 tablespoons frozen orange
concentrate, thawed, warmed

Combine the flour, sugar and salt in a bowl.

In another bowl, beat the egg until light. Add the milk and vanilla and stir into the dry ingredients. Stir until smooth, then let stand for 1 hour.

Cover the apricots with boiling water and let stand until cool. Chop the apricots into small dice. Combine with the honey, butter and orange rind in a small saucepan. Bring to a boil and cook until thick, stirring frequently. Set aside to cool.

Lightly oil a nonstick skillet or crepe pan. Make 8 to 12 5-inch crepes, cooking them 1½ minutes on one side and 30 seconds on the flip side. Spread out on wax paper to cool.

Place about 1½ tablespoons of filling on the light side of each crepe and roll up. Place the crepes side by side in a lightly buttered baking-serving dish. Cover with a lightly buttered piece of aluminum foil.

Before serving, reheat for 5 to 10 minutes in a 400° F. oven. Sprinkle very lightly with sugar and a little warmed orange concentrate.

Turkey Thigh Chili

YIELD: 4 TO 6 SERVINGS

1 turkey thigh
2 tablespoons safflower or corn oil
1 large onion, chopped
2 carrots, sliced
1 green pepper, seeded and chopped
1 large clove garlic, minced
1 pound can plum tomatoes

3 cups chicken stock
2-3 tablespoons Pecos® all-natural ground hot chili
2-3 tablespoons Pecos® all-natural ground mild chili
1 teaspoon ground cumin
1 cup Monterey Jack cheese, shredded

Using a sharp knife, remove the skin from the turkey thigh and cut out the bone, scraping the knife along the bone to loosen from the meat. Save the bone. Cut the meat into large cubes.

Heat the oil in a large saucepan and saute the onion, carrots, pepper and garlic just until coated on all sides. Add the tomatoes with the juice, the chicken stock, the chiles and the cumin. Cook uncovered until the turkey shreds easily and the sauce is quite thick—1½ to 1¾ hours.

Season to taste, adding salt or salt substitute as desired. Top with shredded cheese. Serve with Hy-Ly Tex Mex Cornbread or surround with a good supply of taco corn chips.

Hi-Ly Tex Mex Corn Bread

YIELD: 4 TO 8 SERVINGS

1 cup high-lysine cornmeal
2 teaspoons baking powder
½ teaspoon salt (optional)
2 eggs
6 drops Tabasco

1 stick corn oil margarine, melted
1 cup sour cream
1 package (10 ounces) frozen corn, thawed
4 ounces sharp cheddar, sliced

Preheat the oven to 375° F. Put the dry ingredients in the electric mixing bowl and start the beater. Add the eggs, Tabasco, melted margarine and sour cream and beat until thoroughly blended. Fold in the corn kernels.

Vegetable-spray a 9-inch square pan and pour in half the batter. Cover with the cheese slices and top with the rest of the batter, spreading it with a spatula. Bake 35 to 40 minutes.

Hi-Ly Fried Tomatoes

YIELD: 4 SERVINGS

4 large green-red tomatoes
⅔ cup high-lysine cornmeal
Salt (optional)
Freshly ground black pepper

Tabasco
Corn oil
Parsley, chopped

Wash the tomatoes and cut in thick slices. Spread the cornmeal, preferably pulverized in a blender, on a piece of wax paper. Sprinkle with salt, if desired, and plenty of black pepper. Add a few drops of Tabasco.

Dip the slices in the cornmeal, giving them a good thick coating. Let stand 15 minutes.

Heat some oil in a large skillet and brown on both sides. Transfer the cooked slices to a towel-lined baking sheet and keep warm in a 150° F. oven until all the slices are fried. Sprinkle with chopped parsley and serve on a heated platter.

Melon Ball Fruit Salad

YIELD: 4 SERVINGS

2 small ripe canteloupe
2 large ripe peaches
1 bunch seedless white grapes

2 tablespoons frozen orange
 concentrate, thawed
2 teaspoons lemon juice
Mint leaves

Choose melons that are of the same size. Trim each end very slightly so that the melon will sit well on a plate. Chill for not more than 30 minutes.

Peel and slice the peaches. Combine with the stemmed grapes, the orange concentrate and lemon juice. Cover and chill until serving time. If the peaches are very ripe there will be no need of sugar.

At serving time divide the fruit between the melon halves and garnish with a mint sprig.

Luncheon Party

Fish Fillets Supreme

Sliced Tomatoes, Herb Vinaigrette

Hi-Fiber Sally Lunn
(see Breads and Basics)

Carrot Raisin Slice
with Ginger Cream Sauce

Fish Fillets Supreme

YIELD: 4 SERVINGS

This is a very inexpensive and pretty party dish that can be prepared ahead of time.

1¼ pounds white fish
1 medium onion
1 stalk celery
1 small carrot
2 teaspoons lemon juice
3 cups water
1 bay leaf
¼ teaspoon powered thyme
½ teaspoon salt (optional)

1 tomato, cut in wedges
4 medium shrimp, cooked
4 black olives, pitted
4 chives
2 hard-cooked eggs, sliced
Lemon wedges
Mayonnaise (See Breads
   and Basics)

Try to buy 4 fillets weighing 5 ounces each. Slice the onion, celery, carrot and combine with the lemon juice, water, bay leaf, thyme and salt if desired in a shallow pan. Bring to a boil. Cover and simmer 15 minutes. Cool completely. Add the fillets and reheat. Barely simmer the fillets for 5 to 6 minutes or until just cooked. Transfer to a rack placed over a shallow pan, to drain. Place in the refrigerator.

Before serving, place the fillets side by side on a lettuce-lined platter. Spread each with an even coating of mayonnaise and garnish with the 2 halves of a shrimp split horizontally and 2 olive halves. Dip the chives in boiling water for 10 seconds and twine them between the shrimps and olives. Arrange the egg slices alternating with tomato and lemon wedges between the decorated fish fillets.

Sliced Tomatoes, Herb Vinaigrette

YIELD: 4 SERVINGS

6 ripe tomatoes
1 bunch watercress
2 cloves garlic, minced
2 tablespoons parsley, chopped
2 tablespoons tarragon vinegar

2 tablespoons olive oil
3 tablespoons safflower oil
¼ teaspoon black pepper
Salt, if desired

Wash and slice the fresh tomatoes. Place them in the center of a rectangular platter each slice overlapping the next.

Remove the hard stems and any wilted leaves from the watercress. Wash and dry. Surround the tomatoes with the watercress. Sprinkle the tomatoes with the garlic and parsley.

Combine the vinegar, oils, pepper and a dash of salt, if desired, in a glass jar and shake to mix well.

Spoon the sauce over the tomatoes and serve.

Carrot Raisin Slice with Ginger Cream Sauce

YIELD: 4 SERVINGS

Carrot Raisin Bread (see Breads
   and Basics)
1 cup low-fat cottage cheese
1 tablespoon brown sugar

1 teaspoon vanilla extract
2 tablespoons candied ginger,
   diced

Make the bread a day in advance. Cut in ½-inch slices and place on individual dessert plates.

To make the topping, spin the cottage cheese, sugar and vanilla in a food processor until very smooth. Fold in the finely diced ginger. Chill well.

To serve: Top the bread slices with the ginger cream.

DINNERS

Fish and fowl are featured here, since dinner is traditionally the high protein meal of the day. Chicken, turkey, and halibut are all good sources of complete proteins that are also low in fat. High-fiber ingredients are used more subtly at dinner time, but nevertheless they are present in delicious forms, for better health and nutrition. Some of these recipes call for the high-lysine cornmeal to be pulverized in the food processor, to give a smoother texture.

Menu: Dinner I

Raw Mushroom and Crab Salad

Halibut with Sweet Sour Sauce

Steamed Spring Potatoes

Hot Spinach Salad

Hi-Ly Italian Cornmeal Dessert Cake

Raw Mushroom and Crab Salad

YIELD: 4 SERVINGS

½ pound crab meat
¼ pound fresh white mushrooms
2 teaspoons lemon juice
8 black olives

Cottage Cheese Dressing
  (see Breads and Basics)
2 tablespoons chives, chopped
Lettuce leaves

Line small individual salad plates with lettuce leaves. Inspect the crab meat to be sure there are no hard filaments.

Carefully wipe any soil particles from the mushrooms. Trim the stems and slice through both cap and stem in very thin slices. Spread on a plate and sprinkle with lemon juice.

Cut the olives in half, removing the pits.

Prepare the dressing (see Breads and Basics).

Shortly before serving, line small individual salad plates with lettuce leaves. Put a mound of crab meat in the center of each plate, making a round depression in the center of the crab meat with the bowl of your spoon. Surround the crab with mushroom slices. Place some dressing in each little depression and garnish with the black olives. Sprinkle chopped chives on tops. Serve the rest of the dressing in a separate bowl.

Halibut with Sweet Sour Sauce

YIELD: 4 SERVINGS

Make the sauce in advance. It can be quickly reheated at your convenience.

Sauce:
2 large sweet onions
4 tablespoons corn oil margarine
1 cup cider vinegar
1 teaspoon oregano
2 tablespoons sugar

½ teaspoon black pepper, freshly
ground
Salt (optional)
1¾ pounds halibut steaks
Juice of 1 lemon
2 tablespoons corn oil

To make the sauce: Slice the onion very thin. Saute in the heated margarine until soft. Add the vinegar, oregano, and sugar. Stir well and cook down until the sauce has a syrupy consistency. Season to taste with plenty of black pepper and salt (if desired).

Brush each steak on both sides with oil, and sprinkle with lemon juice. Grill over charcoal or bake 12 to 14 minutes on a preheated rack in a roasting pan in a 375° F. oven. Place the pan 4 inches from the broiler so that the fish can be browned for the last few moments by turning on the broiler, if the fish is not sufficiently browned in baking. Do not over cook.

Place the steaks on a sizzling hot platter and cover with the sauce.

Steamed Spring Potatoes

YIELD: 4 SERVINGS

Place 8 to 12 new pink potatoes, of approximately the same size, in a steamer over boiling water. Steam 25 minutes or until tender.

Serve around the halibut steaks.

Hot Spinach Salad

YIELD: 4 SERVINGS

2 pounds fresh spinach

2 tablespoons onion, minced

2 tablespoons tarragon vinegar

3 tablespoons safflower oil

Black pepper, freshly ground

Salt (optional)

2 eggs, hard-cooked

Pick over the spinach removing the roots and hard stems. Wash very carefully. Place in a large kettle. Add ¼ cup of water or just let the spinach steam in the water clinging to the leaves. Cover and cook 8 to 10 minutes or until just tender.

Drain and place in a serving bowl. Cut coarsely with a sharp knife. Add the onion, vinegar, oil, pepper and salt, if desired. Toss well with a salad fork and spoon. Garnish with sliced hard-cooked eggs.

Hi-Ly Italian Cornmeal Dessert Cake

YIELD: 4 TO 6 SERVINGS

4 tablespoons golden raisins

4 tablespoons dark raisins

1 cup boiling water

1 cup milk

½ cup sugar

½ teaspoon salt (optional)

½ cup high-lysine cornmeal

1 cup all-purpose unbleached flour

4 tablespoons unsalted butter

2 eggs

½ cup citron, finely diced

Grated rind of 1 lemon

1 teaspoon vanilla

1½ teaspoons baking powder

Confectioners sugar

Preheat the oven to 350° F. Lightly grease a small angel cake pan. Soak the raisins in boiling water.

Scald the milk over moderate heat. Stir in the sugar and salt, if desired. Gradually add the cornmeal and flour, stirring constantly with a wooden spoon until smooth and well blended. Remove the pan from the heat. Stir in the butter and when it has melted add the eggs, one by one, beating hard after each addition.

Drain the raisins and squeeze them dry in paper toweling. Add them, the citron and the lemon rind. Stir in the vanilla and finally stir in the baking powder. Mix quickly and pour the batter into the prepared pan.

Bake for 40 to 45 minutes or until golden brown and an inserted cake tester comes out clean. Turn upside down to cool. When cool enough to remove from the pan, sprinkle with confectioners sugar. Cool completely before cutting.

Italian Antipasto

YIELD: 4 SERVINGS

An Italian meal often starts with an antipasto which is a kind of mini salad buffet. It takes very little preparation other than shopping, but there must be variety, and colors are important.

8 thin leeks
1 small can roasted red peppers
4 eggs, hard-cooked
4 large mushrooms
1 can tuna fish
2 teaspoons parsley, chopped
8 anchovy fillets
1 small can pickled beets
Greek or Italian olives
Lettuce leaves

Vinaigrette:
3 tablespoons red wine vinegar
½ teaspoon Dijon mustard
3 tablespoons corn or safflower oil
1 tablespoon olive oil
1 tablespoon anchovy oil
½ teaspoon salt or salt substitute
Several grinds of black pepper
3 tablespoons sweet basil,
  chopped

Trim the leeks taking off all but an inch of the green. Wash well and boil for 10 to 12 minutes or until tender. Drain and cool.

Slice the roasted pepper into thin strips. Peel and quarter the eggs. Wash the mushrooms briefly and slice lengthwise.

Drain the anchovies, reserving the oil for the dressing. Drain the tuna and divide into 4 wedges. Chop the parsley to sprinkle on the tuna. Slice the beets.

Make the Vinaigrette by combining the listed ingredients.

To assemble: Put 2 leeks in the center of lettuce-lined large salad plates. Garnish decoratively with red pepper strips. Surround the leeks with clumps of the prepared ingredients and spot here and there with olives.

Just before serving, spoon the Vinaigrette over the leeks, the mushrooms, tuna and beets.

Chicken Hi-Ly Polenta

YIELD: 4 SERVINGS

1½ cups high-lysine cornmeal
4½ cups water
½ teaspoon salt (optional)
2 chicken breasts (skinless and boneless)
2 tablespoons olive or corn oil
2 tablespoons parsley, chopped

1 can (14½ ounces) tomato puree
8 tablespoons onion, minced
1 teaspoon sweet basil, chopped
2 tablespoons unsalted butter
Black pepper and salt (optional)
Parmesan cheese, freshly grated

Bring the water to a boil in the top part of a double boiler. Gradually add the cornmeal, whisking constantly to keep the mixture from lumping. Add the salt, if desired. When well blended, cook over simmering water for 1 hour, stirring from time to time to keep smooth.

Cut the chicken breasts into large cubes. Saute with the onion in oil in a nonstick skillet until browned on all sides. Add the basil, parsley and tomato puree. Cover and simmer 25 minutes. Just before serving stir in the butter and season to taste with black pepper and a little salt if desired.

Spread half the cooked cornmeal (the polenta) in a heated shallow bowl or platter. Cover with half the sauce. Spread the remaining polenta over the sauce and cover with the remaining sauce. Sprinkle heavily with Parmesan cheese and serve with an extra bowl of Parmesan.

Fiddlehead Salad

YIELD: 4 SERVINGS

Fiddleheads are becoming very popular. They are the tender shoots of a wild fern that is now cultivated widely. Bright green in color, they taste a little like asparagus.

1 pound fiddleheads
1 clove garlic, minced
3 tablespoons red wine vinegar
4 tablespoons safflower or corn oil

1 tablespoon olive oil
2 teaspoons dill, chopped
½ teaspoon salt (optional)
¼ teaspoon black pepper

Throw the fiddleheads into a large pan of boiling water. Bring to a boil and boil 1 minute. Pat dry with toweling.

Combine the remaining ingredients and, just before serving, toss the fiddleheads with the dressing.

Poached Pears with Raspberry Sauce

YIELD: 4 SERVINGS

4 large firm ripe pears
3 cups water
1 stick cinnamon
2 cloves
1 teaspoon lemon peel, grated
1 tablespoon honey

Stuffing:
6 tablespoons apricots, finely chopped
1 tablespoon honey
1 package (10 ounces) frozen raspberries, thawed
Mint leaves

Peel the pears, leaving the stems on. Cut off a very thin slice from the bottom of the pear so that it will sit evenly on a plate. Core the pear from the bottom, making a cavity large enough to hold the filling.

Put the water, cinnamon stick, cloves, lemon peel and honey in a skillet or broad-based pan. Bring to a boil and carefully put in the pears. Return to a boil and simmer 8 to 10 minutes or until just tender.

Remove from the pan with a slotted ladle and let the pears drain on a rack while cooling. Chill in the refrigerator. Mix together the honey and chopped apricots.

Reserve a few raspberries and puree the rest in a food processor or a blender. Strain out the seeds, if desired.

Place 1½ tablespoons of the apricot mixture into the cavity from the bottom. Spread some of the raspberry puree in the bottom of 4 dessert plates. Stand the pears in the sauce and place mint leaves on top of the pears. Garnish with the reserved berries.

Corn Crepes with Chicken Livers

YIELD: 4 SERVINGS

Crepes:
2 eggs
½ cup milk
1 cup fresh or frozen corn kernels
3 tablespoons whole wheat pastry
  flour
½ teaspoon salt (optional)

Chicken Liver Filling:
½ pound chicken livers

3 tablespoons corn oil margarine
1 large shallot, minced
¼ cup white wine vinegar
1 teaspoon Dijon mustard
1½ cups chicken stock
1 tablespoon arrowroot
¼ teaspoon white pepper
½ teaspoon salt (optional)
2 tablespoons heavy cream
Parsley, chopped

To make crepes: Beat the eggs and milk together until well blended. Add the corn, pastry flour and salt, if desired. Mix until the batter is smooth. Cover and let stand 1 hour.

Heat a 5-inch crepe pan or a large skillet and brush lightly with corn oil. Drop 5-inch crepes on the skillet and let cook 1½ minutes or until the surface is full of little holes. Turn and cook 30 seconds on the other side. Stack on a plate as the crepes are cooked. These can be made in advance and reheated briefly in the oven. This recipe will make 8 crepes.

To make chicken liver filling: Trim all fat from the livers, separating the lobes. Heat 2 tablespoons of margarine in a skillet. Saute the livers over moderately high heat, stirring gently until browned all over but still slightly pink inside. Remove from the pan with a slotted spoon.

Add the remaining margarine to the skillet and when heated add the shallots and saute just until soft. Add the wine vinegar and stir with a fork until the mixture boils. Add the mustard and the chicken stock and reduce by ½ over moderately high heat. Dissolve the arrowroot in 2 tablespoons of cold water and stir into the mixture. When the sauce has thickened add the pepper and salt, if desired. Put in the livers and add the cream. Reheat but do not boil.

To serve: Fill each crepe with the chicken livers and sauce and serve two on individual heated plates. Sprinkle with chopped parsley.

Stuffed Tomato Salads

YIELD: 4 SERVINGS

4 tomatoes
1 3-ounce package cream cheese
¼ cup celery, chopped
1 tablespoon parsley, minced

1 tablespoon soy sauce
4 teaspoons mayonnaise
1 large avocado

Choose medium large tomatoes that are about the same size and shape. Dip them in boiling water to loosen the skins and then peel. Hollow out the rounded side, removing all seeds. Place upside down on a rack to drain.

Mix together the cream cheese, celery, minced parsley, soy sauce and mayonnaise. Divide into 4 equal portions. Roll each portion into a ball and place it inside a tomato. Peel, seed and slice the avocado.

To serve, place the tomatoes on individual lettuce-lined salad plates and top each with a little more mayonnaise. Arrange the avocado slices around the tomatoes.

Baked Peaches

YIELD: 4 SERVINGS

4 large firmly ripe peaches
4 candied cherries
½ cup prunes, finely diced
1 teaspoon lemon rind, grated

2 teaspoons corn oil margarine
4 teaspoons frozen lemonade
  concentrate, thawed

Preheat the oven to 350° F. Vegetable-spray a baking/serving dish large enough to accommodate 8 peach halves.

Slice one of the cherries into thin strips and set aside. Chop the remaining cherries with the prunes until they almost form a paste. Mix with the lemon rind and the margarine.

Dip the peaches into boiling water for 30 seconds and slip off the skins. Halve the peaches and remove the stones. Place the peaches cut-side up in the dish. Fill centers with cherry/prune mixture. Spoon the lemonade concentrate over the peaches and bake for 15 minutes. Cool.

Serve at room temperature—not chilled. Garnish with the reserved cherry slices.

Cucumber Yogurt Soup

YIELD: 4 1-CUP SERVINGS

1 medium to large cucumber
1 green onion (scallion)
1 tablespoon onion, minced
2 tablespoons green pepper,
  chopped
½ teaspoon garlic, minced
1½ tablespoons tamari (soy sauce)
1 tablespoon lemon juice
1 quart tomato juice
2 cups Vegetable Broth (see
  Breads and Basics)

2 cups yogurt
Pepper, freshly ground
4 tablespoons fresh parsley,
  chopped
1 teaspoon each:
  celery seed, chopped dill weed,
  fresh marjoram, or oregano,
  fresh thyme, fresh minced basil,
  fresh chopped parsley, fresh
  chopped chives

Wash and halve the cucumber and remove the seeds with a spoon. Do not remove the skin unless it is thick. Slice as thin as possible into a large bowl.

Prepare the onions, green pepper, and garlic; and combine with the cucumber. Measure out the herbs. If fresh herbs are not available, use half the amount
of the dried variety. Mix with the vegetables. Add the tamari and lemon juice and mix well.

Finally add the tomato juice, Vegetable Broth and yogurt. Chill in the refrigerator until just before serving.

Serve in individual bowls, garnished with parsley. Accompany with strips of toasted whole wheat bread.

Small Roast Turkey with Herbed Corn Bread Stuffing

1 small turkey (8 to 10 pounds)
1 carrot, sliced
1 bay leaf
1 sprig thyme

Stuffing:
2 tablespoons corn oil margarine
2 tablespoons onion, minced

2 tablespoons celery, minced
4 cups Herbed Corn Bread Stuffing
(see Breads and Basics)
1 cup dried bread crumbs
1 tablespoon poultry seasonings
(optional)
Chicken broth
½ cup heavy cream (optional)

Rinse the turkey inside and out with cool water. Dry well with paper toweling.

To make giblet broth: simmer the giblets and neck with onion, carrot, celery, bay leaf and thyme in 4 cups of water for 1½ hours.

To make the stuffing: Heat the margarine and saute the onion and celery just until soft. Combine the Herbed Corn Bread Stuffing Mix and the dried bread crumbs in a bowl. Stir in the margarine mixture. Season to taste with pepper and salt (if desired). If you like stuffing highly spiced, add the extra tablespoon of poultry seasoning. Toss, adding enough chicken broth to give the desired moistness.

Shortly before cooking fill the cavity two-thirds full with the stuffing. Close the opening with lacing pins and kitchen twine. Truss the bird and place it on a rack in an open roasting pan. Rub with the oil.

Roast in a preheated roasting oven at 400° F. for 20 minutes. Reduce the heat to 350° F. and continue cooking for 3 to 3½ hours. The turkey is cooked if the juices run clear when pricked in the thigh with a fork. When the turkey starts to brown, cover it with a foil tent. Baste the bird frequently.

To make thin gravy: Pour off all but 2 tablespoons of fat from the pan. Add the giblet broth and bring to a boil, stirring the gravy with a fork to loosen the juices. Boil down a little before straining into a gravy bowl. The addition of ½ cup heavy cream will give a richer gravy.

Zucchini and Carrot Crustless Pie

YIELD: 4 TO 6 SERVINGS

2 medium zucchinis
2 medium carrots
2 tablespoons corn oil
3 tablespoons onions, chopped
1 teaspoon oregano
2 tablespoons whole wheat pastry
   flour

1 egg
⅔ cup low-fat milk
½ teaspoon salt (optional)
6 drops Tabasco
4 tablespoons sharp cheddar
   cheese, grated

In advance, wash the zucchini and scrub the carrots very clean. Cut both vegetables into sticks, approximately 1½ inches long and ¼ inch thick. Bring a shallow pan of water to a full boil. Throw in the zucchini. Return to the boil and cook 2 minutes. Remove from the pan with a slotted spoon and rinse in cold water. Drain and spread on toweling to dry.

Throw the carrot sticks into the same pan and boil them 5 minutes. Drain, rinse in cold water, drain and spread out to dry.

Heat the corn oil and saute the onions 1 minute without browning. Add the vegetable strips and oregano. Stir until well coated. Cover and cook 5 minutes. Transfer to a 9-inch shallow baking/serving dish.

Preheat the oven to 350° F. Beat the egg, milk and seasonings until well blended. Pour over the vegetables and sprinkle with cheese. Bake 40 minutes.

Strawberry Cheese

YIELD: 4 SERVINGS

Make this a day in advance.

1 pound cottage cheese
2 tablespoons milk
4 tablespoons brown sugar

1 pint wild or small cultivated
   berries
4 tablespoons light honey
½ teaspoon cinnamon

Spin the cottage cheese, milk and sugar in a food processor until very smooth. Place in a strainer lined with cheese cloth and suspend it over a bowl. Chill in the refrigerator for 24 hours, so that it will chill completely.

Hull the berries. If only large berries are available, cut them into quarters. Mix with the honey and cinnamon. Cover and chill.

To serve: Unmold the cheese onto a dessert platter and pour the sauce over the cheese.

Menu: Dinner V

Avocado and Grapefruit Salad

*Turkey Bourgignon and
Whole Wheat Noodles*

Broccoli With Lemon Chive Topping

Cottage Cheese Tortoni

Avocado and Grapefruit Salad

YIELD: 4 SERVINGS

1 head garden lettuce
1 large ripe avocado
1 can grapefruit sections packed
in their own juice

4 tablespoons scallions, chopped
(white and green parts)
Herb Vinaigrette (see Breads
and Basics)
4 large stuffed olives, sliced

In advance, wash the lettuce leaves and shake them very dry.

Peel the avocado and cut into thin wedges. Place in a bowl with the grapefruit sections and 4 tablespoons of the juice. Add the chopped scallions and ½ cup of the Herb Vinaigrette. Chill.

Just before serving, line a salad bowl with the lettuce leaves and put the avocado mixture in the center. Sprinkle with the olives. Toss at the table.

Turkey Bourgignon and Whole Wheat Noodles

YIELD: 4 SERVINGS

1 turkey thigh (1¾ pounds)
2 tablespoons corn oil
1 medium large onion, chopped
1 medium large carrot, sliced thick
1 clove garlic, pressed
½ pound mushrooms, sliced
1¼ cups Chicken Stock (see Breads and Basics)

¼ cup red wine vinegar
1 teaspoon salt (optional)
Bay leaf and herbs
½ teaspoon black pepper, freshly ground
2 tablespoons corn oil margarine
12 ounces whole wheat noodles
2 tablespoons parsley, chopped

Remove the skin from the turkey thigh and cut off the meat. Cut into large cubes. Reserve the bone.

Heat the oil in a heavy pan. Saute the turkey cubes, stirring until lightly browned on all sides. Reduce the heat and remove the cubes with a slotted spoon.

Cook the onion in the pan until soft. Do not brown. Add the carrot, garlic, chicken stock and the wine vinegar. Bring to a simmer and add the turkey and the mushrooms and enough boiling water to just come to the top of the ingredients. Add the seasoning.

Cover tightly and simmer very slowly for 3 hours. Remove the cover just before serving and stir in the margarine.

Cook the noodles in rapidly boiling water for 10 minutes. Drain well and pile in the center of a heated platter. Cover with the Turkey Bourgignon and sprinkle with the chopped parsley.

Broccoli with Lemon Chive Topping

YIELD: 4 SERVINGS

1 large bunch broccoli
2 tablespoons corn oil margarine
4 tablespoons toasted bread crumbs
1 tablespoon chives, minced

1 egg, hard cooked, chopped
Salt (optional)
White pepper
2 teaspoons lemon juice

Trim the broccoli of leaves and cut off the hard stem ends. Split the stems in half lengthwise to ensure even cooking. Rinse well. Steam or boil until tender (10 to 15 minutes).

Meanwhile heat the margarine in a small saucepan. Toss the bread crumbs and chives in the margarine until well coated and lightly browned. Remove from the heat and stir in the lemon juice and the chopped egg, tossing lightly with a fork. Season to taste. Keep warm.

Drain the broccoli thoroughly and place in a heated vegetable dish. Spread the topping over the broccoli and brown 1 minute under a preheated broiler.

Cottage Cheese Tortoni

YIELD: 4 SERVINGS

2 cups low-fat cottage cheese
¼ cup light brown sugar
3 tablespoons golden raisins
2 tablespoons candied cherries,
  minced

2 tablespoons candied orange
  peel, minced
1 teaspoon vanilla
3 tablespoons vanilla wafers,
  pulverized

Spin the cottage cheese in a food processor until smooth. Put in a strainer and let it drain over a bowl in the refrigerator for several hours.

Fold in the sugar, fruits and vanilla and pack into 4 invididual souffle cups or custard cups. Smooth the tops. Sprinkle generously with the cooky crumbs. Chill several hours before serving.

Quick Spanish Gazpacho

YIELD: 4 TO 6 SERVINGS

½ **pound Hi-Ly Peasant Bread (see Bread and Basics)**
1 **medium sized cucumber**
1 **large onion**
2 **cloves garlic, peeled**
1 **green pepper, seeded and sliced**
1 **quart tomato juice**
4 **tablespoons red wine vinegar**
3 **tablespoons corn oil**
2 **tablespoons olive oil**

⅛ **teaspoon Tabasco**
⅛ **teaspoon black pepper**
Salt to taste (optional)

Garnish:
2 **eggs, hard cooked**
1 **cucumber, diced**
½ **sweet red pepper, minced**
Parsley, chopped

Tear the bread in large pieces into a bowl. Cover with cold water. Prepare the vegetables and puree them in a food processor or blender.

Squeeze the water out of the bread and add to the bowl along with 2 cups of the tomato juice. Process that and then feed through the tube the vinegar and oils, Tabasco and pepper.

Pour into a 2-quart container. Add the rest of the juice and taste for seasoning. Chill before serving.

Chop the eggs quite fine and put in a small bowl. Serve the remaining garnishes in separate bowls.

Chicken Supremes with Wild Rice

YIELD: 4 SERVINGS

4 large chicken breasts	3 cups chicken stock
16 to 24 raw shrimp	4 tablespoons corn oil margarine
1 cup wild rice	4 tablespoons whole wheat pastry
White pepper	flour
2 tablespoons shallots, chopped	2 tablespoons corn oil margarine
Basil and thyme	¼ cup heavy cream (optional)

Ask your butcher to split each breast horizontally and to pound each half into a cutlet. Otherwise do the operation yourself. It is very simple. Pound each piece between wax paper using a meat pounder or a mason jar to flatten thin.

Shell and clean the shrimp, saving the shells. Wash the rice well and pour it slowly into 4 cups of boiling water. Cover and simmer 40 to 45 minutes or until tender.

Season each cutlet very lightly with white pepper. Place chopped shallots and 2 or 3 raw shrimp, depending on size, in the center and sprinkle lightly with basil and powdered thyme. Roll up tightly and secure with a small skewer or with kitchen twine. At the same time put the shrimp shells in the chicken stock. Cover and simmer 10 minutes.

Remove the cover and boil down until it measures about 2 cups. If any shrimp remain, simmer them in the stock for 2 minutes. Strain the broth through a fine sieve. Discard the shells, but save the shrimp for garnish.

Heat 2 tablespoons of margarine in a skillet. Saute the chicken rolls until lightly browned on all sides. Remove to a shallow baking-serving dish. Add the remaining margarine and when heated stir in the flour. Cook gently for 2 minutes before whisking in the chicken-shrimp broth. Whisk until smooth and thickened. Pour over the cutlets. Bake in a 350° F. oven for 25 minutes.

Heat the margarine in a small pan. Strain the rice thoroughly and toss with the margarine. Pile the rice in the center of a heated platter. Surround with the chicken rolls. Taste the sauce for seasoning, adding the cream, if desired. Reheat but do not boil.

Pour a small spoonful of sauce on each roll and serve the rest in a separate heated bowl.

Carrots in Mustard Broth

YIELD: 4 SERVINGS

8 long thin carrots
2 teaspoons Dijon mustard
1 tablespoon corn oil

2 summer savory leaves
1 tablespoon chives, chopped
⅛ teaspoon white pepper

Cut off the stem ends of the carrots and scrape them lightly. Cut in 1½-inch pieces and put in a pan of lightly salted cold water. Bring to a boil and cook 20 to 25 minutes or until just tender.

Remove the carrots to a bowl and boil down the cooking liquid until it measures ⅔ cup. Stir in the mustard, the corn oil, the finely chopped savory leaves and the chives. Season with the pepper and pour over the carrots. Reheat just before serving.

Sparkling White Fruit Coupe

YIELD: 4 SERVINGS

1 small ripe cantaloupe
1 small bunch seedless grapes
1 small can mandarin oranges
1 small cup pineapple chunks

Juice of ½ lemon
I bottle sparkling grape
　juice, chilled

Scoop out the melon with a small melon ball cutter and combine with the grapes in a bowl. Drain the oranges and the pineapple and boil down the juice to half its original quantity. Set aside to cool and add the lemon juice.

Cut the canned fruits into small pieces so that all the fruit will fit comfortably into tulip shaped wine glasses. Pour the cooled syrup over the fruit and keep cool but not chilled.

Just before serving, fill the glasses with the fruit and pour over the sparkling chilled grape juice.

SPECTACULAR SEAFOOD ENTREES

Because it is a good source of complete protein, high in lysine, low in sodium and fat—and low in calories—fish deserves a chapter of its own in any collection of healthful recipes. If you think fish is boring, it may be because you meet it only broiled or grilled, with the conventional sprig of parsley and wedge of lemon as its only companions. Try the recipes in this collection—they will introduce you to a whole new world of exquisite and delectable seafood dishes. One of the blessings of modern technology is the network of rapid transportation that makes fresh seafood available in nearly all parts of the country today. Take advantage of this largess!

Swordfish with Onion Sauce

YIELD: 4 SERVINGS

1½-2 pounds swordfish steak
(1 inch thick)
2 cups onion, thinly sliced
3 tablespoons corn oil margarine
½ cup cider vinegar

2 tablespoons honey
1 teaspoon oregano
½ teaspoon salt (optional)
⅛ teaspoon black pepper

Preheat the broiler. Cut fish into 4 portions. Place on a baking sheet greased with a little margarine. Paint with 1 tablespoon of margarine.

Heat the remaining margarine in a skillet and saute the onions until soft, stirring frequently. Add the vinegar, honey, oregano, and seasonings. Stir well. Cover and simmer 10 to 15 minutes. Keep warm.

Place the baking sheet 4-6 inches from the broiler. Broil 5 to 6 minutes on each side. Transfer to a very hot platter and remove the skin. Cover with the onion sauce.

Grilled Tuna with Tomato Sauce

YIELD: 4 SERVINGS

4 6-ounce tuna steaks (1 inch thick)
2 tablespoons corn oil
2 tablespoons red wine vinegar

Sauce:
2 tablespoons corn oil margarine
1 medium size onion, chopped

1 tablespoon garlic, chopped
½ teaspoon rosemary
1 can (12 ounces) Italian plum
tomatoes, chopped
1 cup beef broth
1 teaspoon tomato paste

Place the steaks on a lightly greased baking sheet. Mix the oil and vinegar and spread over the fish pressing lightly with your finger tips. Let stand 30 minutes or longer in the refrigerator.

Heat the margarine in a skillet. Saute the onion until soft. Add the garlic and cook 1 minute. Add the rosemary, tomatoes and beef broth, mixed with the tomato paste. Bring to a boil and simmer, partially covered for 30 minutes. Season as desired.

Broil the tuna 5 minutes on each side, placing the pan 6 inches from the broiler. Transfer to a hot platter and cover with the sauce.

Tuna Casserole with Water Chestnuts

YIELD: 4 SERVINGS

1 cup fresh bread crumbs
1 cup shredded sharp cheddar
  cheese
3 tablespoons corn oil margarine
2 tablespoons onion, chopped
3 tablespoons flour

1½ cups milk
1 can tuna
1 can sliced water chestnuts
2 teaspoons Worcestershire sauce
Tabasco

Preheat the oven to 400° F. Crumb 2 slices slightly stale, firm white bread in the processor. Shred the cheese.

Heat the margarine in a saucepan and saute the onion until soft. Stir in the flour and cook slowly for 2 to 3 minutes, covered.

Whisk in the milk and cook until slightly thickened. Add the tuna and chestnuts and season with Worcestershire and Tabasco. Mix well.

Pour into a lightly greased 1½ quart baking-serving dish. Spread with the crumbs and bake 20 minutes. Top with the grated cheese and bake until the cheese is melted and lightly browned.

Parslied Winter Flounder

YIELD: 4 SERVINGS

Winter flounder is one of the best of the flounder family and is usually seen in the market during the winter months. If unavailable, substitute sole fillets.

8 small (2 ounce) winter flounder
   fillets
3 tablespoons corn oil margarine
2 tablespoons shallots, chopped

2 tablespoons parsley, chopped
½ cup water
1 teaspoon lemon juice

Preheat the oven to 400° F. Choose fillets of equal size.

Heat 2 tablespoons of the margarine in a skillet and saute the shallots until soft. Stir in the parsley and cook 1 minute longer.

Melt the remaining margarine. Spread in the bottom of an oven-proof serving dish, large enough so that the fish can be placed in a single layer over the margarine. Mix the water and lemon juice, pour over the fish and cover with the shallot-parsley mixture. Cover with parchment paper which has been lightly covered with margarine. Bake 6 minutes. Remove the foil and sprinkle with the remaining fresh parsley.

Fillet of Sole, Somerset

YIELD: 4 SERVINGS

2 tablespoons corn oil margarine
2 tablespoons shallots
4 large fillets of sole
   (4-5 ounces each)
1 cup water
1½ teaspoons lemon juice

¼ pound mushrooms, sliced
½ teaspoon salt (optional)
⅛ teaspoon white pepper
4 tablespoons mayonnaise
2 tablespoon chives, chopped
1 tablespoon parsley, chopped

Heat the margarine and saute the shallots just until soft. Spread over the pan and put the fillets in one layer. Mix the water and lemon juice and pour over the fish. Spread the mushrooms over the fish. Cover and simmer 8 to 10 minutes or until the fish flakes when penetrated with a fork.

Transfer the fish with a slotted spatula to a heated platter. Turn up the heat under the skillet and boil down to about ½ cup. Season to taste. Heat mayonnaise without letting it boil. Spread over each fish fillet and sprinkle with the chives and parsley. Surround the fillets with the mushrooms and sauce.

Baked Haddock, French Style

YIELD: 4 SERVINGS

4 haddock fillets (5-6 ounces) equal shape and weight
2 tablespoons shallots, chopped
½ pound white mushrooms, sliced thin
¼ cup celery, finely diced
⅔ cup chicken stock (see Breads and Basics)
2 teaspoons lemon juice
⅔ cup whipping cream
Italian bread crumbs
2 tablespoons corn oil margarine
1 tablespoon lemon juice
Salt (optional)
White pepper

Preheat the oven to 425° F. Grease a baking-serving dish large enough to accommodate the fish fillets in a single layer.

Prepare the vegetables and mix them together. Spread the mixture in the bottom of the dish. Season lightly with salt, if desired, and with pepper. Cover the vegetables with the fish, placed side by side.

Mix the chicken stock, lemon juice and cream and pour gently over the fish. Sprinkle with the seasoned bread crumbs and dot with margarine. Bake 10 to 15 minutes, according to the thickness of the fillets. The fish should flake slightly when penetrated with a sharp knife. Sprinkle with lemon juice just before serving.

Baked Halibut Steak, Fine Herbes

YIELD: 4 SERVINGS

1½ pounds halibut steak (¾-1 inch thick)
Juice of ½ lemon
4 tablespoons corn oil margarine
2 tablespoons shallots, chopped
3 tablespoons parsley, chopped
1 tablespoon dried dill
Salt (optional)
Black pepper, freshly ground

Preheat the oven to 400° F. Line a small baking sheet with aluminum foil. Paint the sheet with 2 tablespoons of melted margarine and sprinkle with half the shallots, parsley and dill. Sprinkle with salt, if desired and plenty of freshly ground black pepper.

Place the fish on the herbs. Paint with the remaining margarine and cover with the rest of the herbs. Cover with another sheet of foil and roll the edges to seal in the juices.

Bake 35 to 40 minutes. Remove the top sheet 10 minutes before the end of cooking time. Drain off any excess liquid. Invert the steak onto a heat proof serving platter sprinkle with juice of ½ lemon, and brown under a boiler.

Salmon Mousse with Dill Mayonnaise

YIELD: 4 TO 6 SERVINGS

This is pretty molded in a cup fish mold. It makes an elegant luncheon dish or can be served as the first course of a dinner party.

2 tablespoons shallots, chopped	Salt (optional)
2 tablespoons corn oil margarine	White pepper
2 cups chicken broth	1 cucumber, thinly sliced
1 pound fresh salmon	1 black olive
3 tablespoons powdered gelatin	
¼ cup plain yogurt	Sauce:
6 tablespoons cream	1 cup yogurt
¼ cup unseasoned mayonnaise	¾ cup unseasoned mayonnaise
2 tablespoons lemon juice	1 teaspoon dill, freshly chopped

Saute shallots in margarine in a pot. Add the chicken broth and the salmon and cook gently for 10 to 12 minutes or until the salmon flakes when you insert a fork. Remove the salmon from the broth and cool. Strain the broth through a very fine sieve and set aside to cool.

Remove the skin and bones from the cooled salmon. Put the salmon in a food processor with 4 tablespoons of the reserved broth. Spin until smooth.

Boil ½ cup of the reserved broth. Dissolve the gelatin in 3 tablespoons of cold broth. Stir the dissolved gelatin into the boiling broth. Place in the refrigerator 5 minutes and stir frequently.

Combine the salmon mixture, yogurt, cream, and mayonnaise. Mix until blended with a wooden spoon. Season with lemon juice, salt (if desired), and white pepper. Spoon into a lightly-oiled fish mold and smooth evenly with a spatula. Cover with plastic wrap and refrigerate at least 3 hours.

Make a simple sauce by combining a cup of yogurt with ¾ cup of unseasoned mayonnaise and flavored with a teaspoon of freshly chopped dill.

Shortly before serving unmold the salmon on a platter. Surround it with thinly sliced cucumber and give the salmon 2 eyes with thin slices of black olive.

Braised Sole with Vegetables

YIELD: 4 SERVINGS

1½ pounds sole fillets (thick)
2 tablespoons corn oil margarine
1 large onion, sliced thin
2 carrots, sliced thin
2 stalks celery, sliced
1 teaspoon salt (optional)

8 white peppercorns
1 cup water
1 teaspoon white wine vinegar
1 cup fish or chicken stock
1 bay leaf
1 tablespoon parsley, chopped

Preheat the oven to 425° F. Heat the margarine in an oven-serving dish over medium heat. Saute the onion, carrots and celery until the onion is soft and the carrots crisply tender.

Put the fish on the vegetables. Sprinkle lightly with salt, if desired, and dot with the remaining margarine. Add the peppercorns and pour the acidulated water stock around the fish. Place the bay leaf on the fish. Cover tightly and bake 15 minutes.

Remove the bay leaf and sprinkle with chopped parsley. Serve with boiled potatoes.

Easy Baked Sea Scallops

YIELD: 4 SERVINGS

1 pint sea scallops (cut in half)
6 tablespoons corn oil margarine
1 cup whole wheat cracker crumbs

1 tablespoon lemon juice
4 lemon wedges
Parsley, chopped

Heat the margarine in a medium size skillet. Add the cracker crumbs and stir until well coated. Remove the pan from the heat and stir in the scallops. Place in a baking serving dish. (This can all be prepared up to this point in advance. Keep refrigerated until baking time.)

Twenty minutes before serving, sprinkle with the lemon juice and bake at 350° F. Serve with lemon wedges and sprinkle with the chopped parsley.

Shrimp Stuffed Potatoes

YIELD: 4 SERVINGS

4 Idaho baking potatoes
2 egg yolks
2 tablespoons corn oil margarine
2 tablespoons onion, chopped
½ pound raw shrimp, shelled
   and cleaned

¾ cup drained Italian tomatoes
¾ cup whipping cream
⅛ teaspoon nutmeg
Tabasco

Scrub the potatoes well and prick them in several places. Bake 50 minutes in a conventional oven (20 minutes in a microwave). Cut off ⅓ inch from a long side of each potato.

Scoop out the insides of the potatoes into a mixing bowl. Mash with 1 tablespoon of margarine, ¼ cup of cream and the yolk of 1 egg. Season with a little salt, if desired, and white pepper.

While the potatoes are baking, prepare the shrimp sauce: Saute the chopped onion in the remaining margarine, using a medium skillet. Add the well drained Italian tomatoes, cut into ¼ inch dice. Simmer 3 minutes. Add the shrimp and cook 2 minutes, tossing or stirring frequently. Add the remaining cream and simmer very gently for 5 minutes. Season with nutmeg and Tabasco.

Fill the potatoes with the shrimp mixture. Pipe the potatoes around the rim using a ⅓ inch cannelated tip. Brown lightly under a preheated broiler.

New England Fish Chowder

YIELD: 4 TO 6 SERVINGS

2 pounds haddock fillet
1 pound fish trimmings (head,
   tail & bone)
Bay leaf
Thyme
2 tablespoons corn oil margarine

1 medium onion, diced
2 cups potatoes, diced
2 cups milk
Salt (optional)
Freshly ground black pepper

Keep the fillets in the refrigerator. Cover the bones and trimmings with 2 cups of water. Add a bay leaf and a little thyme and simmer 20 minutes. Strain. Discard the fish trimmings.

Heat the margarine in a saucepan. Saute the onion until soft. Add the potatoes and cover with the fish stock. Simmer until the potatoes are just tender.

Cut the fish fillets into large bite-size pieces. Add to the stock and simmer very gently for 10 minutes. Add the milk and bring to just below the simmering point. Cook without boiling for 5 minutes.

Season to taste. Be generous with the pepper. Remove from the heat and let stand overnight if possible. Chowder is always best the second day. Refrigerate when cool.

Whitefish and Crab Salad

YIELD: 4 SERVINGS

This is a great way to use left-over fish. It's a good idea to cook enough fish when you are serving it for dinner to allow for left-overs.

3 cups cooked white fish (cod, haddock, halibut, etc.)
½ pound crabmeat

Sauce:
1 small bunch watercress

Large handful of spinach leaves
1 clove garlic, pressed
1½ cups bland mayonnaise
2 teaspoons lemon juice
1 onion, sliced thin
Lettuce leaves

Flake the fish and crabmeat with your fingers to be sure there are no bones or shell. Keep them separate.

Spin the watercress leaves, spinach leaves and garlic in a food processor. Add the mayonnaise and lemon juice and spin 2 seconds longer.

Spread a layer of sauce on a serving platter and mound the fish in the center. Spread the sauce over the fish and smooth it into a nice shape. Cover the mound with the crabmeat and spoon a little of the mayonnaise on the top. Surround the mound with little lettuce leaves and garnish with onion rings and more of the mayonnaise.

Poached Salmon, Caper Sauce

YIELD: 4 SERVINGS

1½ pounds tail end of salmon
2 quarts water
2 cups red wine vinegar
1 onion stuck with 2 cloves
1 small carrot, sliced
1 stalk celery
½ teaspoon thyme
1 bay leaf
4 sprigs parsley

Sauce:
1 egg yolk
1 teaspoon caper juice
1 teaspoon white wine vinegar
½ cup corn oil
Salt (optional)
White pepper
1 tablespoon capers

Wrap the salmon in a piece of cheesecloth large enough so that there are 2 long ends with which to retrieve the salmon from the *court-bouillon*.

In a pan large enough to accommodate the fish, combine the water, vinegar, onion, carrot slices, celery and herbs. Bring to a boil. Cover and simmer 20 minutes. Cool to lukewarm.

Lower the fish into the pan and bring to a simmer. Cook very gently for 10 minutes or just until the fish flakes. Remove the fish from the liquid and unwrap it. Remove the skin. Using a spatula, lift off the top half and transfer it to a heated platter. Remove the bones and transfer the lower half and place it along side the top half. Cover with the caper sauce.

Caper Sauce
Put the egg yolk with the juice from the bottle of capers and a teaspoon of wine vinegar in a blender. Add 1 tablespoon of oil and spin briefly. Start adding the oil in a very fine stream and spin until the mixture thickens. Remove to a small bowl and add desired seasonings and the capers. Serve with small boiled (unskinned) spring potatoes.

Sauteed Perch, Anchovy Sauce

YIELD: 4 SERVINGS

Anchovy Butter:
2-3 anchovy fillets
4 tablespoons corn oil margarine
⅛ teaspoon lemon juice
8 perch fillets (1-1¼ pounds)

Milk
Flour
Corn oil
Lemon wedges
Parsley sprigs

Combine the anchovies, margarine and lemon juice in a blender or food processor and spin until blended. Keep at room temperture.

Dip the fillets in milk and then in flour. Heat ⅛ inch of oil in a skillet and when very hot add the fish. Brown on one side (not more than 2 minutes). Turn and brown on the other side.

Transfer to a heated platter and spread each one with anchovy butter. Garnish with lemon wedges and sprigs of fresh parsley. Serve very hot.

Curried Fish Pudding

YIELD: 4 SERVINGS

1 pound thick fish fillets (haddock, ocean perch, halibut, monkfish)
1 tablespoon vinegar
½ cup brown rice
2 tablespoons corn oil margarine
10-12 medium size cooked shrimp

2 tablespoons parsley, chopped
2 eggs
1¾ cups milk
Tabasco
½ teaspoon salt (optional)
2 teaspoons curry powder

Cook the fish in simmering water to cover. Add a tablespoon of vinegar. When tender, remove the fish from the water with a slotted spoon. Let cool. Flake the cooled fish. Meanwhile, boil or steam the brown rice until tender (40 to 45 minutes). Fluff the rice with the margarine, using a fork.

Shell and clean the shrimp. Preheat the oven to 350° F.

Lightly grease a 2 quart baking dish. Put in a third of the cooked rice. Cover with a layer of flaked fish and top with half the shrimp. Sprinkle with chopped parsley. Repeat the process and top with a layer of cooked rice.

Beat the eggs and milk until tender. Add a few drops of Tabasco (according to taste), the salt (if desired), and the curry powder. Mix well. Pour over the layers. Bake 50 minutes.

TEST KITCHEN FAVORITES

In the sparkling new test kitchen that adjoins the offices of the *Post Society* our staff stirs, simmers and bakes, trying out new products and new ways of preparing old-favorite foods. Always, the emphasis is on healthful cuisine: using natural high-fiber ingredients, little oil or none at all, fresh fruits and vegetables when available, seasoning with herbs and garlic rather than salt. High-lysine cornmeal, triticale, amaranth, barley and Ezekiel flour (a special blend of wheat, barley, pinto beans, lentils, millet and rye), are some of the ingredients we have used in the new recipes presented here. We think you will enjoy trying these recipes, and that you will be inspired to experiment, as we do, changing and adapting recipes to suit our individual preferences. Cooking is—or should be—a creative art. Enjoy!

Homemade Chips and Dip

Corn chips:
1 cup high-lysine cornmeal
½ cup unbleached flour
¼ teaspoon baking soda
¼ teaspoon salt (optional)
¼ teaspoon paprika
⅓ cup milk
2 tablespoons corn oil

Guacamole Dip:
1 large or 2 small avocados
1 tablespoon onion, chopped
2 tablespoons lemon juice
Salt (optional
Pepper to taste
1 or 2 canned green chili
    peppers (optional)

Combine all the ingredients for the corn chips and work together with a stiff dough. Divide into four parts for easier handling. Shape each into a ball, then flatten and roll between sheets of wax paper until as thin as pie crust. Cut into rectangles approximately 1- by 2-inch and bake on an ungreased cookie sheet, 15 minutes at 350° F.

For the guacamole dip, combine all the ingredients in a blender and spin until smooth. Taste and correct seasonings. Spoon into a small bowl, cover with plastic wrap and chill in the refrigerator at least 2 hours before serving.

Chicken Macaroni

YIELD: 6 SERVINGS

3 cups whole-wheat macaroni,
    cooked
2 cups chicken, cooked, chopped
1 can (16 ounces) tomatoes,
    chopped and juice
1 cup celery, chopped
1 cup green pepper, chopped

1 cup carrots, grated
¼ cup chives, chopped
¼ cup parsley, chopped
1 teaspoon fresh ginger, grated
    (optional)
Black pepper to taste
1 cup chicken or vegetable stock

Combine all ingredients in an oven-proof dish. Cover and cook in a 350° F. oven for 30 to 40 minutes or until well heated all the way through.

Apple and Green Pea Salad

YIELD: 4 SERVINGS

3 Jonathan apples
1 cup peas, cooked tender
1 cup celery, diced
¼ cup green pepper, chopped
2 tablespoons onion, grated

½ cup cheddar cheese, diced
Mayonnaise
Lemon juice
Lettuce

Peel, core and dice the apples. Combine with the peas, celery, green pepper, onion and cheese. Stir in 2 tablespoons lemon juice, then just enough mayonnaise to bind. Taste for seasoning, adding more lemon juice if it seems flat. Chill for at least 4 hours before serving on lettuce-lined salad plates.

Fish and Spinach Casserole

YIELD: 6 TO 8 SERVINGS

6 to 8 fillets (flounder, snapper,
  haddock, pompano, etc.)
Salt (optional) and pepper
4 tablespoons corn oil margarine
Chicken stock
2 pounds fresh spinach
Parmesan cheese, grated

Cream Sauce:
4 tablespoons corn oil margarine
4 tablespoons flour
1 cup spinach broth
1 cup milk
⅛ teaspoon nutmeg

Season the fillets with salt (optional) and pepper. Melt 4 tablespoons corn oil margarine in a large skillet. Add enough chicken stock to measure ½ inch in the skillet. Bring to a boil. Poach the fillets for just 5 minutes, spooning the chicken stock over the fish. Remove from the liquid.

Wash the spinach removing the large stems. Put in a large pan, cover and cook until tender. Drain and reserve the broth.

Prepare cream sauce: Heat 4 tablespoons corn oil margarine in a saucepan. Add the flour and cook 2 minutes, stirring with a whisk. Add the spinach broth and bring to a boil, stirring constantly. Add the milk and whisk until smooth and thickened. Season with the nutmeg and, if desired, a little salt and pepper.

Preheat the oven to 350° F. Spread half the cream sauce in the bottom of a baking-serving dish. Place the fish fillets on the sauce. Cover with the spinach and pour over the remaining sauce. Sprinkle with grated cheese and bake 20 minutes.

Tropical Chicken Salad

YIELD: 6 SERVINGS

1 apple
1 orange
1 cup seedless grapes
1 cup pineapple, fresh or canned,
   cut into small pieces

½ cup celery, diced
2½ cups cooked chicken, diced
Yogurt Fruit Salad Dressing
   (see Breads and Basics)

Core and dice the apple; do not peel. Peel the orange, divide into segments, and remove the white membrane.

Combine the apple, orange pieces, pineapple pieces, celery and cooked chicken in a glass or china bowl. Add dressing to taste (about ¾ cup); cover tightly and chill in the refrigerator.

If you prefer, substitute mayonnaise thinned with a little pineapple juice for the yogurt dressing.

Millet Bread

YIELD: 1 LOAF

1 cup plain yogurt
½ cup corn oil margarine
1 tablespoon honey
1 package dry yeast

¼ cup warm water
2 eggs
2 cups millet flour
½ cup soy flour

Combine yogurt and margarine in saucepan, heating slowly to melt margarine. Dissolve honey and yeast in the warm water; add yogurt mixture and blend. Beat in eggs; add flours and beat well. Pour into well-oiled loaf pan and let rise for 45 minutes. Bake at 375° F. for 40 to 45 minutes or until done.

High-Lysine Cornmeal Waffles

YIELD: 4 WAFFLES

1 cup high-lysine cornmeal
1 cup whole wheat flour
2 teaspoons baking powder

2 tablespoons margarine, melted
1⅓ cups low-fat buttermilk
1 egg and 1 egg white

Blend together in mixing bowl the cornmeal, flour and baking powder. Make a well in the center and add buttermilk, egg and egg white. Stir just to moisten the flour. Beat in melted margarine. Five rounded tablespoons make one waffle.

Creamy Barley Mushroom Soup

¾ cup pearled barley
1 large onion, chopped
1 large carrot, chopped
2 bay leaves
2 tablespoons margarine
2½ cups water or vegetable stock
1 medium potato, diced
1 large celery, finely chopped
¼ cup parsley, chopped

1 teaspoon dried dill weed
½ teaspoon dried summer savory
1 teaspoon salt (optional)
½ teaspoon pepper
½ pound fresh mushrooms, chopped
2 cups milk
2 tablespoons barley flour

Place barley, onion, carrot, bay leaves and margarine in a large pot with water or vegetable stock. Bring to a boil, cover and simmer over low heat for 10 minutes.

Remove bay leaves. Add potato, celery, parsley and seasonings. Cover and simmer for 15 minutes.

Add mushrooms and milk, cover and simmer over very low heat for about 20 minutes or until vegetables are tender but not overdone.

Dissolve the flour in just enough water (½ cup or 125 ml.) to make a smooth, flowing paste and whisk it quickly into the soup. Allow the soup to stand for 5 to 10 minutes off the heat before serving. It thickens if it is refrigerated. Add more milk or water as needed and adjust the seasonings.

Millet Chili Pie

YIELD: 4 TO 6 SERVINGS

Crust:
1 cup millet
¼ cup high-lysine cornmeal
4 cups water
1 teaspoon onion powder
½ teaspoon chili powder

Chili Filling:
1 cup onion, sliced
½ cup green pepper, chopped
1 cup mushrooms, sliced
1 tablespoon corn oil margarine
1 can (15 ounces) kidney beans, rinsed and drained
1 can (28 ounces) low-sodium tomatoes, drained

1 can (4 ounces) low-sodium tomato sauce
1 teaspoon chili powder
1 teaspoon cilantro (optional)
½ teaspoon garlic powder
½ teaspoon cumin
½ teaspoon curry powder
½ teaspoon blackstrap molasses
¼ teaspoon cayenne pepper
Oat bran
1 can (8 ounces) corn, drained
1 cup olives, sliced and divided
1 cup low-fat cheese, grated
½ cup Monterey Jack cheese, grated

Preheat oven to 350° F.

To make the crust: Combine the millet, cornmeal, water, onion powder and ½ teaspoon chili powder in a double boiler. Cook 25 to 30 minutes over boiling water, until thick and stiff. Set aside ¾ cup of the crust mixture for topping. Use the rest to line the bottom and sides of a 2-quart casserole.

To make the filling: Saute the onion, green pepper and mushrooms in the margarine, until tender. Add the kidney beans, tomatoes, the tomato sauce and the seasonings. Cover and simmer for 30 minutes. If there is much liquid left after the chili simmers, thicken it with the oat bran. Stir in 1 teaspoon at a time until almost no liquid is left.

Add the corn, ½ cup of the olives, and the low-fat cheese. Stir until the cheese melts, then pour the chili filling into millet-lined casserole. Top with the Monterey Jack cheese and spread the rest of the millet mixture on top. Bake about 30 minutes, then garnish with the remaining olives.

Corn Bread Bean Bake

YIELD: 6 SERVINGS

Taco Sauce:
2 cups tomato sauce
1 or 2 whole tomatoes
4 tablespoons vinegar
1 teaspoon garlic powder
½ teaspoon cumin
½ teaspoon basil
1 small can of green chilies,
 chopped
Dash of Tabasco (optional)
1 hot dried pepper, crushed
 (optional)

Cornbread Batter:
1 cup whole wheat flour
¾ cup high-lysine cornmeal
2 teaspoons baking powder
1 egg plus 1 egg white
1 cup skim milk
2 tablespoons corn oil

4 cups pinto beans, cooked
1 small onion, diced
2 cups low-fat cheddar cheese,
 grated

To make the taco sauce: Process the whole tomatoes in the blender.
Combine with all the other ingredients and heat in a saucepan. Simmer
20 minutes to blend seasonings.

 To make the cornbread batter: Combine and mix the dry ingredients in
one bowl. Combine the egg, egg white, milk and corn oil in another bowl and
stir them into the dry ingredients, just until moistened.

 Spread the cooked pinto beans in the bottom of a 9-inch by 13-inch baking-
serving dish. Spread the onions over the beans, then the cheese over all. Top
with 2 cups of the taco sauce (freeze any leftover sauce) and drop the
cornbread batter on, by spoonfuls. Bake in 350° F. oven for 30 minutes.

Cornmeal Pancakes

YIELD: 4 SERVINGS

½ cup high-lysine cornmeal
½ cup whole wheat flour
1 teaspoon baking powder
⅓ cup buttermilk

1 egg
1 tablespoon margarine, melted
2 tablespoons cranberry-orange
 relish for topping

Blend together in mixing bowl the cornmeal, flour and baking powder.
Make a well in the center and add buttermilk and egg. Beat just to moisten the
flour. Beat in melted margarine. Bake on nonstick griddle.

Hearty Spinach Patties

YIELD: 4 SERVINGS

For the patties:
2 tablespoons shallots, minced
3 tablespoons bulgur
⅓ cup unsweetened apple juice
1 cup well-drained spinach,
   cooked, chopped
½ cup well-packed bean sprouts,
   dried and chopped
½ cup toasted wheat germ
½ cup low-sodium Swiss cheese,
   grated

½ teaspoon nutmeg, freshly grated
¼ cup low-fat plain yogurt
4 light dashes cayenne pepper
Salt to taste (optional)
1 tablespoon corn oil margarine

For the garnish:
½ cup low-fat plain yogurt
2 tablespoons Mrs. Dash® salt
   free 14-herbs-and-spices blend

Combine shallots, bulgur and apple juice in small, nonstick skillet or saucepan. Bring to boil. Cover and simmer for 5 minutes. Remove from heat and let stand for 5 minutes. Turn into bowl. Blend in balance of ingredients, except margarine, one at a time, and blend thoroughly after each addition. Shape mixture into 8 3-inch patties.

    Heat margarine in large, nonstick skillet until melted but not brown. Saute patties over medium-high heat until browned on both sides. Serve with garnish on the side.

Crunchy Banana Bread

1 cup unbleached flour
1 cup triticale flour
1½ teaspoons baking powder
½ teaspoon soda
½ teaspoon salt (optional)
¼ cup corn oil margarine, melted

¾ cup skim milk
½ cup banana, mashed
1 tablespoon honey
½ teaspoon vanilla
⅓ cup Grape-Nuts® Cereal

Mix dry ingredients in a large bowl. Add margarine, skim milk, banana, honey and vanilla. Mix until moistened, then stir in cereal. Pour into a loaf pan which has been oiled. Bake in a 375° F. oven for 30 minutes or until done. Refrigerate to keep fresh.

Bethel Bread

YIELD: 2 LOAVES

4 cups Ezekiel® flour
1 tablespoon coarse sea salt
  (optional)
4 tablespoons of dry active yeast
3 cups warm water (or potato water)

½ cup honey (or less to taste)
2 tablespoons corn oil
¼ cup apple cider vinegar
5 to 5½ cups unbleached
  white flour

In a large mixing bowl combine the Ezekiel® flour, salt and yeast. In a second bowl combine the water, honey, oil and vinegar. Pour the liquid mixture into the dry, and mix thoroughly until thick and creamy. Put in a warm place for 15 minutes for the yeast to work. (A barely warmed oven is good for this.)

Stir in white flour, a cup at a time, mixing thoroughly each time, until too thick to mix. Turn out on floured kneading board and gradually work in the rest of the white flour. When finished the dough should be slightly sticky, not dry.

Oil the inside of the bowl. Then press the dough onto the oiled surface to coat the dough. Turn the oiled side up, cover with a clean damp cloth, and put in a warm place to rise. When dough has doubled the size, punch down, divide in two and form into loaves. Place in oiled or nonstick 5-inch x 9-inch loaf pans and let rise again.

When loaves have increased by about half or so, bake in 350° F. oven for one hour or until nicely browned. (Test for doneness by tapping bottom of loaves for hollow sound.) Cool on rack. Store covered when thoroughly cooled.

High-Lysine Cornmeal Souffle

YIELD: 4 TO 5 SERVINGS

3 cups skim milk
2 tablespoons vegetable oil or
   margarine
1 cup high-lysine cornmeal

1 egg yolk
4 egg whites
¼ teaspoon cream of tartar

Scald the milk. Add the margarine. Slowly add the meal, stirring constantly. Cook 1 minute after adding the last of the meal, still stirring add the beaten egg yolk. Beat the egg whites and cream of tartar until stiff and fold into the cornmeal mixture. Pour into a coated 2-quart casserole. Bake in 350° F. oven for 35 to 40 minutes. Serve immediately.

Cornbean Pie

YIELD: 6 SERVINGS

Crust:
2 cups high-lysine cornmeal
2 tablespoons nutritional yeast
3 tablespoons corn oil
½ cup water and ½ cup
   vegetable stock

Filling:
1 medium-size onion, chopped
½ cup carrots, chopped

½ cup celery, chopped
1 teaspoon garlic powder
½ cup green peppers, chopped
1 cup kidney beans, cooked
1 teaspoon chili powder
1 tablespoon cumin
½ cup tomatoes, chopped
2 tablespoons soy sauce
⅓ cup farmers cheese, grated

Preheat oven to 350° F. Mix together all ingredients for crust and pat into a coated 9-inch pie plate. Saute onion, carrots, celery, garlic and green peppers in oil about 5 minutes. Add beans and spices and put into cornmeal crust. Combine tomatoes with soy sauce and pour over the beans. Bake about 25 minutes. Remove from oven, sprinkle with cheese and bake 5 minutes longer.

Abundance Bran Muffins

YIELD: 2 DOZEN LARGE

2 eggs
3 cups buttermilk
1 cup liquid honey
½ cup corn oil
2½ cups Ezekiel flour

2½ teaspoons baking soda
1 teaspoon sea salt (optional)
1 teaspoon cinnamon
4 cups unprocessed wheat bran
2 cups raisins

Beat eggs in bowl and blend in buttermilk, honey and oil.

Mix together in a second bowl, the Ezekiel flour, baking soda, sea salt, if desired, cinnamon, wheat bran and raisins. Add the liquid mixture to the dry, and mix thoroughly. Place batter in refrigerator for several hours to set.

Oil muffin cups, or use paper liners. Fill ¾ full for regular muffins, or slightly rounded for large ones. Bake 30 minutes in a 350° F. oven. Serve with fruit or applesauce.

Chicken Quiche in Potato Crust

YIELD: 6 SERVINGS

Potato Pastry:
½ cup unbleached white flour
¼ cup triticale flour
½ cup mashed potato
1 egg, beaten
1 tablespoon corn oil margarine

Quiche Filling:
1½ cups chicken, cooked, diced
⅔ cup chicken broth
¼ cup carrot, grated

¼ cup raw potato, grated
2 tablespoons green onion, chopped
1 cup plain yogurt
1 egg yolk, beaten
⅓ cup cheddar cheese, shredded
⅓ cup mushrooms, chopped
¼ teaspoon celery seed, ground
2 egg whites
2 tablespoons Swiss cheese, shredded
¼ teaspoon paprika

To make the crust: Use vegetable nonstick spray to coat a 10-inch pie pan. Combine the ingredients, using leftover mashed potato or one medium potato, cooked and then mashed with a fork. Press the mixture into the pie pan and bake in 350° F. oven for 10 minutes or until golden.

For the filling: Combine all the ingredients except the egg white, the Swiss cheese and paprika. Pour the chicken mixture into the potato crust and bake in 325° F. oven for 45 minutes. Beat egg whites until stiff peaks form. Spread over the quiche. Sprinkle with the shredded Swiss cheese and the paprika. Return to the oven for 10 minutes or until egg white is golden. Cool quiche slightly before serving.

Refrigerator Barley-Bran Muffins

YIELD: 4 DOZEN

2 cups boiling water
6 cups bran flakes
1 cup vegetable shortening
½ cup honey
½ cup brown sugar
½ cup molasses

4 eggs
4 cups buttermilk
5 cups barley flour
5 teaspoons baking soda
2 teaspoons salt (optional)

Pour boiling water over 2 cups of bran flakes; cool slightly. In mixer, on high speed, cream shortening, honey, sugar and molasses. Add eggs and buttermilk and mix well. Sift dry ingredients together and add to wet. Stir until well coated. Add soaked bran and remaining bran and stir well. You may refrigerate batter in covered container and bake as needed. Store up to 4 weeks. Fill well-greased muffin tins ⅔ full. Bake 18 minutes at 400° F.

Barley Bean Salad

YIELD: 6 SERVINGS

¾ cup raw pearled barley
2 tablespoons soy sauce
1 bay leaf
1 cup navy beans, cooked or canned
1 medium cucumber,
    peeled and diced
1 cup green beans, 1″ pieces,
    steamed
⅔ cup sliced black olives
2 tablespoons scallions, minced

2 tablespoons fresh parsley, minced
½ cup plain yogurt
¼ cup olive oil
¼ cup red wine vinegar
½ teaspoon sweet basil
½ teaspoon dried marjoram
½ teaspoon dried dill weed
¼ teaspoon ground pepper
½ teaspoon salt (optional)

Cook the barley (2½ parts water to 1 part barley) and add soy sauce and bay leaf to the cooking water. When the barley is done (about 30 minutes), remove the bay leaf and allow the barley to cool to room temperature.

Transfer barley to a mixing bowl. Add beans, cucumber, green beans, olives, scallions and parsley and mix well. Combine the remaining ingredients in a small bowl and mix thoroughly. Pour over the salad and toss until everything is evenly coated.

This salad can be served immediately or it can stand an hour or so at room temperature or refrigerated.

Cornmeal and Triticale Muffins

YIELD: 12 3-INCH MUFFINS

1 cup high-lysine cornmeal, pulverized
1 cup triticale flour
½ cup unbleached all-purpose flour
½ teaspoon salt (optional)
2 tablespoons brown sugar
2 tablespoons corn oil margarine,
   melted

6 teaspoons baking powder
3 teaspoons onion, minced
2 teaspoons green pepper, minced
2 teaspoons pimiento, minced
½ teaspoon powdered sage
2 eggs, beaten until light
1 cup low-fat milk

Mix all the dry ingredients in a bowl. Prepare the vegetables. Add them and the sage to the beaten eggs, milk and margarine and stir until blended. Pour into the dry ingredients and mix them briefly but thoroughly.

Preheat the oven to 400° F. Prepare tins with margarine or vegetable spray. Fill the tins half-full and bake 20 minutes. Serve with cottage cheese.

High-Lysine Cornmeal/Amaranth Pancakes

YIELD: 16 4-INCH PANCAKES

¼ cup amaranth
1¼ cup high-lysine cornmeal
¼ cup whole wheat flour
1 teaspoon baking soda
½ teaspoon honey

2 cups buttermilk
2 tablespoons corn oil
1 egg yolk, slightly beaten
1 egg white, slightly beaten

Pour boiling water over amaranth (enough to cover grain) and soak for 15 minutes.
Mix dry ingredients. Add drained amaranth. Add buttermilk, oil and egg yolk. Blend well. Fold in egg white. Let stand 10 minutes.
Bake on hot, lightly greased griddle.

Wild Rice Triticale Bread

YIELD: 2 LOAVES

1 package active dry yeast
⅓ cup water, 105° F. to 115° F.
2 cups milk, scalded, cooled to
  105° F. to 115° F.
2 tablespoons corn oil margarine,
  melted
2 teaspoons salt (optional)
½ cup honey

½ cup uncooked rolled oats
2½ cups triticale flour
4-4½ cups unbleached all-purpose
  or bread flour
1 cup cooked wild rice
1 egg, beaten with tablespoon
  water
½ cup hulled sunflower seeds

In large bowl, dissolve yeast in water. Add milk, margarine, salt and honey.
Stir in oats, triticale flour and 2 cups of the bread flour to make a soft dough.
Add wild rice. Cover and let rest 15 minutes.

Stir in enough additional bread flour to make a stiff dough. Turn out onto
a breadboard and knead 10 minutes. Add more flour as necessary to keep dough
from sticking. Turn dough into lightly oiled bowl, turn over, cover and let rise until
doubled, about 2 hours.

Punch down. Knead briefly on lightly oiled board. Shape. Divide entire batch
into 3 parts; shape each into strands, braid and place onto oiled baking sheet to
make a wreath. Or, divide dough into 2 parts; place each into 9½"x5½" oiled
bread pan. Let rise until doubled, about 45 minutes.

Brush tops of loaves with egg mixed with water. Slash loaves, if desired.
Sprinkle with sunflower seeds. Bake at 375° F. for 45 minutes or until loaves
sound hollow when tapped.

Pineapple Casserole

1 egg
1 teaspoon brown sugar
1 teaspoon vanilla
½ teaspoon allspice
2 cups unsweetened,
  crushed pineapple

3 slices whole wheat bread,
  torn in pieces
4 teaspoons bran
Cinnamon

In medium-size bowl, mix egg, brown sugar, vanilla and allspice. Add pineapple and bread. Stir. With slotted spoon, lift into casserole dish, omitting excess liquid. Sprinkle bran and cinnamon on top. Bake in 350° F. oven for 30 minutes.

Fruit Slurry

¾ cup skim milk or or 2% milk
½ banana

2 tablespoons miller's unprocessed
bran

Partially freeze the skim milk until it is slushy before adding other ingredients. Liquefy in the blender for 5 minutes. Serve chilled. The slurries can be varied by substituting ½ cup blueberries or red raspberries for the bananas.

Bran-Apple Betty

⅓ cup miller's unprocessed wheat
  bran
⅓ cup soy granules
½ cup warm water

1 tablespoon lemon juice
1 tablespoon honey
4 medium apples, cored, sliced thin
Cinnamon

Mix bran, soy granules, water, lemon juice and honey in a bowl. Place half of apples in an oiled casserole. Top with half of bran mixture and a sprinkle of cinnamon. Repeat process. Bake covered at 350° F. for 30 minutes. Remove cover and bake an additional ten minutes or until topping is crisp.

Chicken Pie with Corn Bread Topping

YIELD: 6 SERVINGS

4- to 5-pound stewing chicken,
  cut in pieces
1 onion
1 carrot
1 bay leaf
Celery leaves
4 tablespoons corn oil margarine
4 tablespoons flour
¼ teaspoon white pepper
1½ cups green peas, cooked
1½ cups carrots, sliced, cooked
1 cup tiny onions, boiled

Cornbread topping:
1 cup unbleached flour
¾ cup high-lysine cornmeal
½ teaspoon soda
1½ teaspoons baking powder
1 tablespoon sugar
½ teaspoon salt (optional)
1 cup buttermilk or sour milk
2 eggs
3 tablespoons vegetable oil

Place the chicken in a saucepan or a large kettle with 1½ quarts of water with the onion, carrot, bay leaf and celery leaves. Bring slowly to a boil and skim off any froth that appears on top. Add a little salt, if desired, and pepper. Cover and simmer 1 hour or longer, until the chicken is tender. Remove the chicken pieces. Strain the broth and place it in the refrigerator (or freezer, if time is short) to chill. Discard the vegetables and herbs.

When the chicken is cool enough to handle, remove the skin and bones, and all visible fat. Cut the meat into bite-size pieces. Set aside. Skim all fat from the top of the chilled broth. Measure the de-fatted broth and add milk, if needed to make at least 3½ cups. Preheat the oven to 400° F.

Melt the margarine in a heavy saucepan and stir in the flour. Cook 2 to 3 minutes without letting it brown. Stir in half the chicken broth and stir with a whisk until smooth and thick. Add the rest of the broth and stir until blended. Add the cooked chicken, peas, carrots and onions and stir till hot through. Taste for seasoning and add salt and pepper, as desired. Transfer the mixture to a large casserole.

To prepare the topping, combine the dry ingredients in one bowl and the liquids in another. Pour together and mix with a few quick strokes only. Spread the batter 1-inch thick over the casserole and bake 25 minutes or until lightly browned.

Quick and Simple Souffle

YIELD: 2 LARGE OR 4 SMALL SERVINGS

1 tablespoon corn oil
3 eggs, well-beaten
½ cup Ezekiel flour
2 teaspoons baking powder

½ cup milk
½ teaspoon vanilla extract
¼ teaspoon nutmeg

Preheat oven to 450°. Oil iron skillet. Mix beaten eggs, milk, Ezekiel flour, baking powder, vanilla extract and nutmeg thoroughly. Pour batter into skillet and bake for 10 minutes.

Turn souffle and return to oven for 5 minutes more, with burner off. Serve with honey, fresh or canned fruit, maple syrup. Try yogurt with toppings.

Hi-Protein Bran-Fruit Rounds

YIELD: 36 BARS

¼ pound seedless raisins
¼ pound dates
¼ pound pitted prunes
¼ pound figs
1 tablespoon lemon juice
½ cup miller's unprocessed wheat
  bran

½ cup oat bran
½ cup wheat germ
1 tablespoon orange rind,
  grated
¼ teaspoon allspice

Grind fruit in food chopper. Add all other ingredients and mix well. Form into a 12-inch roll. Wrap in wax paper and chill. Slice in ¼-inch rounds and serve.

Amaranth Corn Bread

YIELD: 1 LOAF

1 teaspoon baking soda
1 cup whole wheat flour
1 egg white
¾ cup high-lysine cornmeal

¼ cup amaranth
1 cup buttermilk
1 tablespoon margarine, melted

Sift the baking soda and the flour together. Mix with the other dry ingredients. Beat egg and add it to the milk and the melted margarine. Beat in the dry ingredients, pour into an oiled tin. Bake in a hot oven about 25 minutes.

Victory Garden Pizza

YIELD: 4 SERVINGS

3 medium zucchini, grated (4 cups)
1 egg, beaten
½ cup triticale flour
2 cups low-fat mozzarella cheese, shredded
1 medium onion, diced
1 medium green pepper, diced

1 cup mushrooms, sliced
3 large tomatoes, peeled and thinly sliced
½ teaspoon oregano
½ teaspoon basil
½ cup alfalfa sprouts

Preheat oven to 450° F. Lightly oil a 12- to 14-inch round pizza pan or a 9-inch by 13-inch baking pan. Drain grated zucchini in a colander, pressing out excess liquid, then place into a mixing bowl. Add egg and then flour, blending well. Spread evenly into prepared pan, forming a slight rim around the outside edge. Bake for 8 minutes, or until lightly browned. Remove and reduce oven temperature to 375° F.

Sprinkle half the cheese over the crust. Over this, sprinkle onion, green pepper, and mushrooms. Arrange sliced tomatoes over this, and sprinkle with oregano and basil. Top with remaining cheese. Bake for 20 to 25 minutes, or until set and bubbly. Sprinkle with alfalfa sprouts before serving.

Apples Amaranth

YIELD: 6 SERVINGS

8 apples (cut up), unpeeled
2 tablespoons honey
1 teaspoon cinnamon
¼ cup amaranth flour (make from seeds in blender)

¾ cup water
¼ cup tapioca (quick cooking)
Amaranth seeds, popped

Cook apples in water and drain off excess liquid. Combine apples with honey, cinnamon, flour, water and tapioca. Let stand 5 minutes.

Stir once more and spoon into greased baking dish. Sprinkle popped amaranth seeds lightly on top. Bake 20 minutes at 350° F.

High-Lysine Noodles

1½ cups water
1 cup high-lysine cornmeal
1 tablespoon corn oil magarine
1 egg, beaten

½ cup unbleached flour
1½ teaspoons baking powder
½ teaspoon salt or salt substitute

Bring the 1½ cups water to a boil in a saucepan. Stir in the cornmeal and let stand 5 minutes.

Add the margarine and egg and stir vigorously. Combine the remaining ingredients and stir into the cornmeal mixture, to make a stiff dough. (Add a little more flour if the dough is not stiff.) Let the dough stand, covered, 30 minutes.

Roll the dough on a floured board as for pie crust, very thin. Let stand to dry until stiff but not brittle, then fold and cut into very narrow strips. Let noodles dry thoroughly.

Add to soups or stews, or cook as ordinary noodles.

Green Beans with Artichoke Hearts

YIELD: 6 TO 8 SERVINGS

3-4 cup green beans, cooked,
   drained
1 can artichoke hearts
½ cup low-sodium Italian-style
   salad dressing

¼ cup bread crumbs
¼ cup Parmesan cheese,
   freshly grated

Drain the artichoke hearts and cut them into quarters. Combine with the green beans and the Italian salad dressing. Cover and refrigerate overnight.

A half-hour before serving time, drain the vegetables and spoon them into a greased casserole. Top with the bread crumbs and grated cheese. Bake at 350° F. for 20 minutes, or until heated through.

CANCER PREVENTION REFERENCE

For more detailed information on nutrition and cancer, call the following toll-free telephone number, and you will be connected automatically to the Cancer Information Service Office serving your area:

1-800-4-CANCER*

*In Alaska call 1-800-638-6070; in Washington, D.C. (and suburbs in Maryland and Virginia) call 202-636-5700; in Hawaii, on Oahu call 808-524-1234 (Neighbor Islands call collect).

Spanish-speaking staff members are available to callers from the following areas (daytime hours only): California (area codes 213, 714, 619, and 805), Florida, Georgia, Illinois, Northern New Jersey, New York City, and Texas.

The information listed in this reference section is based on data from *Diet, Nutrition and Cancer Prevention*, published by the U.S. Department of Health and Human Services, Public Health Service, National Institute of Health.

To Increase Your Fiber Intake

CHOOSE **MORE** OFTEN

Whole grain products:
- Bakery products, including whole wheat crackers; **bran** muffins; brown, rye, oatmeal, pumpernickel, bran, and corn breads; whole wheat English muffins, bagels
- Breakfast cereals such as bran cereals, shredded wheat, whole grain or whole wheat flaked cereals, others that list dietary fiber content
- Other foods made with whole grain flours such as waffles, pancakes, pasta, taco shells
- Other foods made with whole grain including barley, buckwheat groats, bulgur wheat

All fruits and vegetables; examples are:
- Apples, pears, apricots, bananas, berries, cantaloupes, grapefruit, oranges, pineapples, papayas, prunes, raisins

- Carrots, broccoli, potatoes, corn, cauliflower, Brussels sprouts, cabbage, celery, green beans, summer squash, green peas, parsnips, kale, spinach, other greens, yams, sweet potatoes, turnips

All dry peas and beans; examples are:
- Black, kidney, garbanzo, pinto, navy, white, lima beans
- Lentils, split peas, black-eyed peas

Snack foods:
- Fruits and vegetables
- Unbuttered popcorn
- Whole grain and bran cereals
- Breads, crackers

CHOOSE **LESS** OFTEN

Refined bakery and snack products:
- Bakery products, including **refined flour** breads, and quick breads, biscuits, buns, croissants, snack crackers and chips, cookies, pastries, pies

To Lessen Your Fat Intake

CHOOSE **MORE** OFTEN

Peas and beans:
- Pinto, black, kidney, garbanzo, navy, white, lima beans; lentils; black-eyed and split peas

Low-fat or skim milk dairy products:
- Low-fat or skim milk and buttermilk
- Low-fat yogurt
- Skimmed evaporated milk, nonfat dry milk*

- Low-fat cheese (ricotta, pot, farmer or cottage, mozzarella, or cheeses made from skim milk)
- Sherbet, frozen low-fat yogurt, ice milk

Fats and oils:
- "Diet" and low-fat salad dressings
- Low-fat margarine

Lower fat poultry, fish, and meat:
- Chicken, turkey, Rock Cornish hens (without skins)
- Fresh, frozen, water-packed canned fish and shellfish
- Reduced fat luncheon meats such as bologna and hot dogs

Beef, veal, lamb, and pork cuts with little or no marbling (visible fat), trimmed of all fat

Infants less than one year old should not be given low-fat or skim milk.

Snack foods:
- Fruits and vegetables
- Breads and cereals

Food preparation:
- Baking, oven-broiling, boiling, stewing (skimming off fat), poaching, stir-frying, simmering, steaming
- Use nonstick cookware to avoid extra fat
- Season vegetables with herbs, spices, or lemon juice

CHOOSE **LESS** OFTEN

Higher fat poultry, fish, and meat:
- Duck and goose
- Poultry with skin
- Frozen fish sticks, tuna packed in oil
- Regular luncheon meats, sausage

Beef, veal, lamb, and pork cuts with marbling, untrimmed of fat

Nuts and seeds:
- Peanut and other nut butters
- Nuts and seeds
- Trail mix

Full-fat dairy products:
- Whole milk
- Butter
- Yogurt made from whole milk
- Sweet cream, sour cream, Half-and-Half®, whipped cream, other creamy toppings (including imitation)
- Full-fat soft cheese such as cream cheese, cheese spreads, Camembert, Brie
- Hard cheeses such as cheddar, Swiss, bleu, American, Monterey jack, Parmesan, etc.

- Ice cream
- Coffee creamers (including non-dairy)
- Cream sauces, cream soups

Fats and oils:
- Vegetable and salad oils, shortening, lard, meat fats, salt pork, bacon
- Mayonnaise and salad dressings
- Margarine
- Gravies, butter sauces

Snack and bakery foods:
- Donuts, pies, pastries, cakes, cookies, brownies
- Potato chips and snack crackers
- Canned puddings, icings, candies made with butter, cream, chocolate
- Granola
- Croissants

Food preparation:
- Batter and deep-fat frying, sauteeing
- Use of fatty gravies and sauces
- Adding cream or butter to vegetables

Reading Food Labels

Many manufacturers list the ingredients and nutrients on their product labels. Food labels often list calories, protein, carbohydrates, fat, vitamins, and minerals per serving. Dietary fiber is sometimes listed on products made from grains. Nutrition information can help you choose foods high in fiber and vitamins A and C and low in fat. Product labels may also list additives and preservatives, but current research does not show these to be strongly linked to cancer risks.

When ingredients appear, they will be listed in order of predominance, starting with the greatest amount and ending with the least. Whole wheat bread, for example, might list 100 percent whole wheat flour as the first ingredient, and a low-fat yogurt would list low-fat milk as the first ingredient. If a cereal lists sugar first, that means the cereal contains more sugar than any other ingredient including grain.

A formula has been developed to help you calculate the percentage of calories in a food product that comes from fat. Because there are nine calories in a gram of fat, the formula is:

$$\frac{\text{grams of fat per serving} \times 9}{\text{total calories per serving}}$$

Here is an example of the formula, using one serving of peanut butter (2 tablespoons) that contains 16 grams of fat and 200 total calories (according to the package label):

$$\frac{16 \ (\text{grams of fat}) \times 9}{200 \ (\text{total calories})}$$

Here is how to calculate it: 16 grams of fat times 9 calories per gram equals 144 calories divided by 200 total calories equals .72 (or 72 percent). So, about 72 percent of the calories in one serving of peanut butter come from fat.

This calculation can be used to identify higher fat foods. To lower fat in your diet, select lower fat alternatives, eat smaller amounts of higher fat foods, or eat them less often. Try to balance your choices of higher fat foods with lower fat ones each day.

The Guide to Reducing Dietary Fat chart is designed to help you decide how many calories from fat and total grams of fat to eat each day. (For example, at 2,000 calories a day, a diet that is 30 percent fat should contain no more than 600 calories or 67 grams from fat.)

Not all food packages list fat content. The Fat and Calories From Some Foods chart provides fat content information for many dairy products, meats, and other foods.

Guide to Reducing Dietary Fat

This guide shows the amount of fat in diets with different proportions of calories from fat. For example, a 2,000 calorie diet calculated to have 30 percent of calories from fat has a total of 67 grams in fat, or 600 calories from fat. Food labels can help you find how many grams of fat are contained in packaged foods.

For a 1,500 calorie diet:

Percent of Calories Desired From Fat	Total Calories From Fat Should Not Exceed	Total Grams of Fat Should Not Exceed
40 percent	600 calories	67 grams
35 percent	525 calories	58 grams
30 percent	450 calories	50 grams
25 percent	375 calories	42 grams
20 percent	300 calories	33 grams

For a 2,000 calorie diet:

Percent of Calories Desired From Fat	Total Calories From Fat Should Not Exceed	Total Grams of Fat Should Not Exceed
40 percent	800 calories	89 grams
35 percent	700 calories	78 grams
30 percent	600 calories	67 grams
25 percent	500 calories	56 grams
20 percent	400 calories	44 grams

For a 2,500 calorie diet:

Percent of Calories Desired From Fat	Total Calories From Fat Should Not Exceed	Total Grams of Fat Should Not Exceed
40 percent	1000 calories	111 grams
35 percent	875 calories	97 grams
30 percent	750 calories	83 grams
25 percent	625 calories	69 grams
20 percent	500 calories	55 grams

BREAKFAST

CHOOSE **MORE** OFTEN

Grain products; especially whole grain types:
- Whole wheat, corn, rye, pumpernickel, and bran breads, muffins, rolls, bagels
- Oatmeal, shredded wheat, bran, flaked, other whole grain cereals
- Whole wheat, bran, corn pancakes, waffles

Low-fat or skim milk dairy products:
- Low-fat or skim milk, skim evaporated milk
- Low-fat yogurt

- Low-fat cheeses like farmer, cottage, and ricotta

Fruits (fresh, canned, juice, or dried); examples are:
- Apples, bananas, apricots, oranges, strawberries, pears, grapefruits, plums, cantaloupes, papayas, tangerines, peaches, berries, watermelons

LUNCH AND DINNER

CHOOSE MORE OFTEN

Vegetable protein sources:
- Lentil, pea, or minestrone soup
- Three-bean salad
- Casseroles and mixed dishes made with garbanzo, kidney, black, pinto, navy, white, lima beans
- Green and black-eyed peas

Low-fat or skim milk dairy products:
- Low-fat or skim milk
- Nonfat dry skim milk
- Low-fat yogurt
- Low-fat cheeses like partially skim milk mozzarella, cottage, farmer, ricotta, "light" processed cheeses
- Sherbet, ice milk, frozen low-fat yogurt

Fish, chicken, and lean meats:
- Water-packed tuna, frozen or fresh flounder, sole, haddock, red snapper, halibut, cod, bluefish, ocean perch, pollack
- Shellfish: shrimp, crab, clams, mussels, scallops

- Chicken, turkey (skinned)
- Beef, lamb, pork, and veal cuts with less marbling (visible fat), trimmed of all fat

Fats and oils:
- "Diet" and low-fat salad dressings
- Yogurt-based dressings

Fruits; examples are:
- Apples, bananas, apricots, oranges, strawberries, pears, grapefruit, plums, raisins, cantaloupes, papayas, tangerines, peaches, berries, pineapples, watermelons, and others

Vegetables; examples are:
- Carrots, broccoli, cauliflower, cabbage, celery, Swiss chard, kale, spinach, romaine, tomatoes, red and green peppers
- Salads containing beans, leafy green lettuce, other greens, any of the vegetables listed above

- Other side dishes, including white and sweet potatoes, eggplant, green beans, squash, asparagus, peas, pumpkin, turnips, Brussels sprouts, corn

Grain products, especially whole grain types:
- Sandwiches made with whole wheat, rye, oatmeal, pumpernickel breads

- Whole wheat pastas

- Barley, bulgur, buckwheat groats, wheat
- Unbuttered popcorn, whole-grain crackers

Food preparation:
- Raw
- Baking, oven-broiling, roasting, microwave cooking
- Stewing, boiling, slow cooking in a crockpot, stir frying, steaming, simmering, poaching
- Frying in nonstick cookware, using no fat

CHOOSE **LESS** OFTEN

Higher fat meats:
- Beef brisket, regular hamburger, rib roasts, corned beef, pastrami, rib and club steaks
- Regular luncheon meats, sausage
- Beef, lamb, pork and veal cuts with marbling, untrimmed of fat
- Meat sauces, gravies, stews and soups containing fat that "cooks out" of meats

Vegetable fat sources:
- Peanut butter
- Nuts, seeds
- Olives

Full-fat dairy products:
- Whole milk
- Butter
- Whole milk yogurt
- Cheeses such as cheddar, American, jack, Swiss, Brie, Camembert, bleu

- Sweet cream, sour cream, Half-and-Half®, whipped cream, other creamy toppings (including imitation)
- Ice cream
- Cream sauces, cream soups

Fats and oils:
- Margarine, mayonnaise, vegetable oils, shortenings, meat fats, gravies, salad dressings
- Potato chips and other fried snacks containing hidden fats

Avocados

Bakery and snack foods; examples are:
- Donuts, pies, pastries, cakes, cookies, brownies, croissants

Food preparation:
- Frying, barbecuing, charcoal broiling, grilling, smoking

Fat and Calories from Some Foods

If you choose to reduce the fat in your diet to 30 percent of your daily calories, for a 2,000 calorie diet that is about 67 grams of fat.

Food	Serv.	Cal.	Grms. Fat	Food	Serv.	Cal.	Grms. Fat
Dairy Products				Lamb, cooked:			
Cheese:				Chops, loin, broiled:			
American,				Lean and fat	3 oz.	250	17
pasteurized proc.	1 oz.	105	9	Lean only	3 oz.	185	8
Cheddar	1 oz.	115	9	Leg, roasted, lean only	3 oz.	160	7
Cottage:				Pork, cured, cooked:			
Creamed	½ cup	115	5	Bacon, fried	3	110	9
Low-fat (2%)	½ cup	100	2	Ham, roasted:			
Cream	1 oz.	100	10	Lean and fat	3 oz.	205	14
Mozzarella, part skim	1 oz.	80	5	Lean only	3 oz.	135	5
Parmesan	1 tbsp.	25	2	Pork, fresh, cooked:			
Swiss	1 oz.	105	8	Chop, center loin:			
Cream:				Broiled:			
Half and Half®	2 tbsp.	40	3	Lean and fat	3 oz.	270	19
Light, coffee, or table	2 tbsp.	60	6	Lean only	3 oz.	195	9
Sour	2 tbsp.	50	5	Pan-fried:			
Ice cream	1 cup	270	14	Lean and fat	3 oz.	320	26
Ice milk	1 cup	185	6	Lean only	3 oz.	225	14
Milk:				Rib, roasted, lean only	3 oz.	210	12
Whole	1 cup	150	8	Shoulder, braised,			
Low-fat (2%)	1 cup	125	5	lean only	3 oz.	210	10
Nonfat, skim	1 cup	85	trace	Spareribs, braised,			
Yogurt, low-fat,				lean and fat	3 oz.	340	26
fruit-flavored	8 oz.	230	2	Veal cutlet, braised			
				or broiled	3 oz.	185	9
Meats				Sausages:			
Beef, cooked:				Bologna	2 oz.	180	16
Braised or pot-roasted:				Frankfurters	2 oz.	185	17
Less lean cuts, such				Pork, link or patty,			
as chuck blade,				cooked	2 oz.	210	18
lean only	3 oz.	255	16	Salami, cooked type	2 oz.	145	11
Leaner cuts, such							
as bottom round,				**Poultry Products**			
lean only	3 oz.	190	8	Chicken:			
Ground beef, broiled:				Fried, flour-coated:			
Lean	3 oz.	230	15	Dark meat with skin	3 oz.	240	14
Regular	3 oz.	245	17	Light meat with skin	3 oz.	210	10
Roast, oven cooked:				Roasted:			
Less lean cuts, such				Dark meat without skin	3 oz.	175	8
as rib, lean only	3 oz.	225	15	Light meat without skin	3 oz.	145	4
Leaner cuts, such				Duck, roasted, meat			
as eye of round,				without skin	3 oz.	170	10
lean only	3 oz.	155	6	Turkey, roasted:			
Steak, sirloin, broiled:				Dark meat without skin	3 oz.	160	6
Lean and fat	3 oz.	250	17	Light meat without skin	3 oz.	135	3
Lean only	3 oz.	185	8	Egg, hard-cooked	1 large	80	6

Food	Serv.	Cal.	Grms. Fat	Food	Serv.	Cal.	Grms. Fat
Seafood				**Other Foods**			
Flounder, baked:				Avocado	½	160	15
With butter or margarine	3 oz.	120	6	Butter, margarine	1 tbsp.	100	12
Without butter or				Cake, white layer,			
margarine	3 oz.	85	1	chocolate frosting	1 piece	265	11
Oysters, raw	3 oz.	55	2	Cookies, chocolate chip	4	185	11
Shrimp:				Doughnut, yeast type,			
French fried	3 oz.	200	10	glazed	one	235	13
Boiled or steamed	3 oz.	100	1	Mayonnaise	1 tbsp.	100	11
Tuna:				Oils	1 tbsp.	120	14
Packed in oil, drained	3 oz.	165	7	Peanut butter	1 tbsp.	95	8
Packed in water, drained	3 oz.	135	1	Peanuts	½ cup	420	35
				Salad dressing:			
Grain Products*				Regular	1 tbsp.	65	6
Bread, white	1 slice	65	1	Low calorie	1 tbsp.	20	1
Biscuit, 2½" across	one	135	5				
Muffin, plain, 2½" across	one	120	4				
Pancake, 4" across	one	60	2				

*Most breads and cereals, dry beans and peas, and other vegetables and fruits (except avocados) contain only a trace of fat. However, spreads, fat, cream sauces, toppings, and dressings often added to these foods do contain fat.

Cruciferous Vegetables

It has been found that vegetables from the cabbage family, known as *cruciferous vegetables*, may reduce your risk of cancer of the colon. As a bonus, cruciferous vegetables are a good source of fiber and certain vitamins and minerals.

Choose several servings each week: Brussels sprouts, cabbage, broccoli, cauliflower, rutabagas, turnips

Fiber Content of Foods

To increase the amount of fiber, choose several servings of foods from the following lists, especially the rich and moderately rich fiber sources. The dietary fiber content of many foods is still unknown, so this is not a comprehensive list of the fiber content of foods. (Fiber content for vegetables and fruits that can be eaten with their skins includes fiber content for the skins.)

Rich Sources of Food Fiber

4 grams or more per serving
(Foods marked with an * have 6 or more grams of fiber per serving)

Breads and cereals	Serv.	Cals. (Rnded to nearest 5)	Legumes (cooked)	Serv.	Cals. (Rnded to nearest 5)
All Bran*	⅓ cup-1 oz.	70	Kidney beans	½ cup	110
Bran Buds*	⅓ cup-1 oz.	75	Lima beans	½ cup	130
Bran Chex	⅔ cup-1 oz.	90	Navy beans	½ cup	110
Corn bran	⅔ cup-1 oz.	100	Pinto beans	½ cup	110
Cracklin' Bran	⅓ cup-1 oz.	110	White beans	½ cup	110
100% Bran*	½ cup-1 oz.	75			
Raisin Bran	¾ cup-1 oz.	85	**Fruits**		
Bran, unsweetened*	¼ cup	35	Blackberries	½ cup	35
Wheat germ, toasted, plain	¼ cup-1 oz.	110	Dried prunes	3	60

Moderately Rich Sources of Food Fiber

1 to 3 grams of fiber per serving

Breads and cereals	Serving	Cals. (Rnded to nearest 5)	Legumes (cooked) and Nuts	Serving	Cals. (Rnded to nearest 5)
Bran muffins	1 medium	105	Chick peas (garbanzo beans)	½ cup	135
Popcorn (air-popped)	1 cup	25	Lentils	½ cup	105
Whole wheat bread	1 slice	60	Almonds	10 nuts	80
Whole wheat spaghetti	1 cup	120	Peanuts	10 nuts	105
40% bran flakes	⅔ cup-1 oz.	90			
Grapenuts	¼ cup-1 oz.	100	**Vegetables**		
Granola-type cereals	¼ cup-1 oz.	125	Artichoke	1 small	45
Cheerio-type cereals	1 ¼ cup-1 oz.	110	Asparagus	½ cup	30
Most	⅓ cup-1 oz.	95	Beans, green	½ cup	15
Oatmeal, cooked	¾ cup	110	Brussels sprouts	½ cup	30
Shredded wheat	⅔ cup-1 oz.	100	Cabbage, red and white	½ cup	15
Total	1 cup-1 oz.	100	Carrots	½ cup	25
Wheat Chex	⅔ cup-1 oz.	105	Cauliflower	½ cup	15
Wheaties	1 cup-1 oz.	100	Corn	½ cup	70

Vegetables continued	Serving	Cals. (Rnded to nearest 5)
Green peas	½ cup	55
Kale	½ cup	20
Parsnip	½ cup	50
Potato	1 medium	95
Spinach, cooked	½ cup	20
Spinach, raw	½ cup	5
Summer squash	½ cup	15
Sweet potato	½ medium	80
Turnip	½ cup	15
Bean sprouts (soy)	½ cup	15
Celery	½ cup	10
Tomato	1 medium	20

Fruits	Serving	Cals. (Rnded to nearest 5)
Apple	1 medium	80
Apricot, fresh	3 medium	50
Apricot, dried	5 halves	40
Banana	1 medium	105
Blueberries	½ cup	40
Cantaloupe	¼ melon	50
Cherries	10	50
Dates, dried	3	70
Figs, dried	1 medium	50
Grapefruit	½	40
Orange	1 medium	60
Peach	1 medium	35
Pear	1 medium	100
Pineapple	½ cup	40
Raisins	¼ cup	110
Strawberries	1 cup	45

Low Sources of Food Fiber

Less than 1 gram of fiber per serving

Breads and cereals	Serving	Cals. (Rnded to nearest 5)
White bread	1 slice	70
Spaghetti, cooked	1 cup	155
Brown rice, cooked	½ cup	90
White rice, cooked	½ cup	80
Corn flake-type cereal	1¼ cup-1 oz.	110

Vegetables	Serving	Cals. (Rnded to nearest 5)
Lettuce, shredded	1 cup	10
Mushrooms, sliced	½ cup	10
Onions, sliced	½ cup	20
Pepper, green, sliced	½ cup	10

Fruits	Serving	Cals. (Rnded to nearest 5)
Grapes	20	30
Watermelon	1 cup	50

Fruit Juices	Serving	Cals. (Rnded to nearest 5)
Apple	½ cup-4 oz.	60
Grapefruit	½ cup-4 oz.	50
Grape	½ cup-4 oz.	80
Orange	½ cup-4 oz.	55
Papaya	½ cup-4 oz.	70

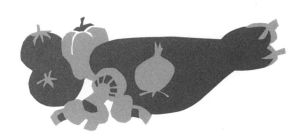

INDEX

Hi-Fiber Cereal Sundae, 30
Hi-Fiber Sally Lunn, 19
Hi-Ly Breakfast Trout, 32
Hi-Ly Cheese Corn Bread, 21
Hi-Ly Crunchy Corn Spoon Bread, 46
Hi-Ly Fried Tomatoes, 49
Hi-Ly Italian Cornmeal Dessert
    Cake, 58
Hi-Ly Mashed Potato Muffins, 23
Hi-Ly Peasant Bread, 18
Hi-Ly Popovers, 22
Hi-Ly Tex Mex Corn Bread, 49
Hi-Ly Whole Wheat Cinnamon Rolls, 24
High-Lysine Cornmeal/Amaranth
    Pancakes, 99
High-Lysine Cornmeal Souffle, 96
High-Lysine Cornmeal Waffles, 90
High-Lysine Noodles, 105
Hi-Protein Bran-Fruit Rounds, 103
Homemade Chips and Dip, 88
Hot Spinach Salad, 58

Italian Antipasto, 59

Kippered Herring with Broiled
    Tomatoes, 33

Mayonnaise, Processor, 27
Melon Ball Fruit Salad, 50
Millet Bread, 90
Millet Chili Pie, 92
Muffins—see Abundance Bran Muffins,
    97; Cornmeal and Triticale Muffins,
    99; Hi-Ly Mashed Potato Muffins, 23;
    Refrigerator Barley-Bran Muffins, 98;
    Savoury Hi-Ly Triticale Muffins, 22

New England Corn Bread Fritters, 37
New England Fish Chowder, 82

Old-Fashioned Johnny Cake, 21
One Egg Omelets, 34
Orange Mint Julep, 34

Orange Prune Whip, 45
Orange Strawberry Mold, 41

Pancakes, High-Lysine
    Cornmeal/Amaranth, 99
Papaya, Fresh Halves with Blue-
    berries, 33
Parslied Winter Flounder, 78
Peaches, Baked, 64
Pears, Poached, with Raspberry
    Sauce, 61
Perch, Sauteed, with Anchovy Sauce, 85
Pineapple Casserole, 101
Pineapple Wedges with Raspberry
    Sauce, 43
Poached Pears with Raspberry
    Sauce, 61
Poached Salmon, Caper Sauce, 84
Polenta, Chicken Hi-Ly, 60
Popovers, Hi-Ly, 22
Potatoes, Shrimp Stuffed, 82
Potatoes, Steamed Spring, 57
Processor Mayonnaise, 27

Quick and Simple Souffle, 103
Quick Spanish Gazpacho, 71
Quick Triticale Corn Bread, 20

Raw Mushroom and Crab Salad, 56
Raw Mushroom Omelet Filling, 36
Refrigerator Barley-Bran Muffins, 98
Rolls, Hi-Ly Whole Wheat Cinnamon, 24

Sally Lunn, Hi-Fiber, 19
Salmon Mousse with Dill Mayonnaise, 80
Salmon, Poached, with Caper Sauce, 84
Sauteed Perch, Anchovy Sauce, 85
Savoury Hi-Ly Triticale Muffins, 22
Shrimp Stuffed Potatoes, 82
Scotch Bannock, 23
Shrimp Creole Omelet Filling, 35
Sliced Tomatoes, Vinaigrette, 52
Small Roast Turkey with Herbed Corn
    Bread Stuffing, 66